D1283778

Real-Life Financial Planning
———— For ————
PHYSICIANS

A Physician's Guide to Financial Security
3rd Edition

Todd D. Bramson, CFP®, CLU®, ChFC®
Wesley R. Sharp
Jon C. Ylinen

ISBN-13: 978-0-578-42817-8

DEDICATION

This book is dedicated to our clients, business partners, staff, and especially our families, without whom we wouldn't have learned the most important lesson of life:

When all is said and done, it is the quality and depth of relationships and experiences that are the essence of life...not the accumulation of material possessions.

THANK YOU

We extend a special thank you to...

- Our clients, who have entrusted us with their financial decisions.

- Our staff, partners, and business associates, who make work a pleasure.

- Attorney Robert Kaufer for his valuable contribution to this book. Bob's insight and knowledge and his ability to communicate information effectively are evident in the estate- planning and asset-protection chapter, which he wrote.

CONTENTS

PREFACE

With more than forty years of combined experience, we have had the privilege of building a unique and specialized financial-planning practice catering almost exclusively to physicians. When asked, "What do you do?" the answer is, on the surface, pretty simple. We consult with residents, fellows, staff, and in-practice physicians, helping them clearly identify their financial goals and objectives. Then we develop a very comprehensive, structured, and coordinated financial plan. Finally, we monitor, review, and update the plan regularly.

However, when you consider the myriad financial decisions and the ramifications these decisions can have on you and your family, it is easy to understand that building and maintaining a sound financial plan is a never-ending and complicated process. As the world becomes more sophisticated and information becomes so accessible, you might assume that making sound financial decisions would be easier than in years past, not more difficult. But sometimes, all the information just makes it more confusing. We help you find the wisdom among the glut of information.

With the bombardment of information, opinions, and advice coming from every angle, it becomes nearly impossible to find the time necessary to fully understand the various financial tools and strategies well enough to make sound decisions. Few occupations require as much time, education, and training as that of a physician. The dedication and commitment required to provide the highest-quality care and stay on top of the ever-advancing field of medicine leaves little time for contemplation of financial decisions.

It is with this understanding that we decided to put our thoughts and experience on paper in an easy-to-read format. In fact, our clients are the ones who suggested we write this book. They told us that these concepts helped them finally understand how to organize and prioritize their financial decisions. Hopefully, this book will help you make sense of the complex world of financial planning as it relates to physicians. We hope you find this resource very helpful.

DISCLOSURE

This information is a general discussion of the relevant federal tax laws. It is not intended for, nor can it be used by, any taxpayer for the purpose of avoiding federal tax penalties. This information is provided to support the promotion or marketing of ideas that might benefit a taxpayer. Taxpayers should seek the advice of their own tax and legal advisors regarding any tax and legal issues applicable to their specific circumstances.

Todd Bramson, Wesley Sharp, and Jon Ylinen offer securities and investment advisory services, including fee-based financial planning, through Securian Financial Services, Inc., and CRI Securities, LLC, affiliates and members FINRA/SIPC.

Separate from the financial plan and our role as financial planners, we might recommend the purchase of specific investment or insurance products or accounts. These product recommendations are not part of the financial plan, and you are under no obligation to follow them.

Additional disclosures are presented in bold type throughout this book.

1

FINANCIAL
GUIDANCE
TAILORED TO
PHYSICIANS'
UNIQUE NEEDS

We have spent more than forty combined years working directly with physicians on their financial plans and financial-planning questions. It often seems that most financial-planning books or publications are written for the average person. Yet physicians have unique needs that necessitate the help of specialists. Hopefully, this book summarizes the wisdom we have learned and shared with our clients in individual meetings through the years. *Real-Life Financial Planning for Physicians* presents a practical method of understanding, organizing, and prioritizing financial decisions.

Most financial-planning publications and financial plans themselves assume that everyone lives a long, healthy life and saves a good portion of their income in quality investments that always do well. This book addresses situations that happen in real life that can interrupt the best-made plans. We hope you take the time to read it and work with a trained professional to develop a financial plan that meets *your* goals and objectives.

WHY SO MANY FINANCIAL-PLANNING BOOKS?

Why is there is an ever-increasing number of financial-planning books on the market today? Because there is an ever-increasing need for people to get educated:

- Few parents openly discuss financial matters with their children while they're growing up.

- Personal financial planning is rarely taught in school. Most physicians spend countless hours educating themselves on their specialties, but very few spend time learning about personal financial planning.

- Most physicians today begin their professional lives already *in the red.* According to the Association of American Medical Colleges, the average medical-school debt for 2016 graduates was $189,000.

- Physicians live high-pressure, busy lifestyles that often allow very little free time to learn about all the options they have.

There are far too many medical specialists today who are ill-equipped to deal with the practical and fundamental necessities of planning for a secure and independent financial life.

FINANCIAL HEALTH REQUIRES THOUGHTFUL PLANNING

Times have changed. Today more than ever, your financial future needs you. Long gone are the days when you could rely on your employer to pay back decades of loyal service with a comfortable pension plan. Certainly, the government can't assure you of a reasonable retirement after a lifetime of Social Security contributions. Not to mention the fact that financial issues have become increasingly complex, and we are continually inundated with confusing financial information.

These facts aren't meant to cause stress, but rather to wake you up to the financial reality that thoughtful planning is needed immediately to help you balance and juggle all the financial decisions you face. You must take control of your decisions, educate yourself, and take steps to use your education and training to set you up for a healthy financial life.

Don't wait another day. This book is meant to give you an introduction to the often-intimidating world of financial planning. You will learn about a variety of investments and insurance options. You will learn the lingo and get practical, "real-life" advice on where to go to next, whether you intend to go the road alone or get some help along the way. Best of all, you will gain ideas to help you climb the pyramid of financial success.

> Financial success isn't the ability to make one or two decisions that turn one dollar into a million.

Financial success isn't, as most people might suspect, the ability to make one or two decisions that turn one dollar into a million. Rather, financial success is the result of many, many small but sound decisions that, when compounded, add up to substantial financial security.

You are in complete control. Or at least you should be.

When it comes to spending, saving, investing, and paying taxes, many people might offer good advice, but you're the only one who can do anything about it. Maybe you're a chronic shopper. Maybe you're unsure of your investment options and how to prioritize them. Maybe you don't have a clue where your paycheck goes each month. In any case, if you're reading this book, you already understand the importance of getting your future under control, and that's the crucial first step to financial freedom.

WHO NEEDS A FINANCIAL PLANNER?

Financial independence and the accumulation of wealth are no accident. Granted, it's not possible to plan for every single event in life, but even tragedy can feel more manageable when you are financially prepared for it. If you're like many people, you probably spend more time *planning for a vacation* than for your entire financial future! Whether it's preparing for the future, securing your family and yourself against tragedy, or planning for the good times, your money deserves your undivided attention.

The truth is, we all need to plan for our financial futures. So the question is not *whether* to plan, but *how* to plan and whether you need a professional to help. The Information Age has intensified the field of financial planning. It is interesting to consider that thirty years ago, financial news might have made top headlines two or three times throughout the year, when the stock market would do particularly poorly or well, or if there was some other major economic news. Today, however, we have news programs dedicated to nothing else 24/7, and the number of financial headlines can be overwhelming. Still, there is a big difference between information and wisdom, and that's where the insight of a trusted professional can help.

SITUATIONS THAT CALL FOR A FINANCIAL PLANNER

The following are some situations that call for a financial planner's expertise:

- **You have no spare time.** If you're working for a large clinic or hospital, it might provide the groundwork for investing wisely for the long term, but even the best can't take into consideration the special circumstances of each individual or family. In this case, a financial planner can save you a bit of your most precious commodity—time.

- **You are easily bored or overwhelmed by financial questions.** If, for example, preparing a budget is such a nuisance that you can't even imagine having to sort through anything more complex, like trends in mutual funds, the stock market, or deciphering insurance options, then hiring a financial planner might be money well spent for greater financial confidence.

- **You are considering a complicated set of employee benefits in combination with personally owned insurance and investments.** You certainly don't want a new employer (or an existing employer that has changed its benefit structure) to conflict or overlap with your current investments. Such gaps or possible duplications should be examined thoroughly.

- **You are recently divorced or have lost a spouse who handled financial affairs for the household.** As if dealing with the trauma of divorce or death is not enough, being thrown into unknown financial waters without a trusted advisor can make you feel like you're trying to stay afloat with bricks chained to your ankles.

- **You recently finished your residency or fellowship and are suddenly thrust into making many important and critical decisions.** The saying "An ounce of prevention beats a pound of cure" is an important one in the world of financial planning. Seemingly insurmountable debt plagues the future of many physicians and surgeons. Budgeting properly, choosing from insurance options, and making wise investments are necessary life skills. Getting professional advice now beats paying for costly mistakes later.

- **You are running or plan to start your own private practice.** In this case, you most likely have to "wear many hats" as an entrepreneur. You are in sales, accounting, customer service, personnel, and oh, yeah…practicing medicine. You probably don't have time to investigate or be aware of the many planning options available for you and your employees. A financial planner can help you sort through the many issues you face.

TRUST YOUR OWN JUDGMENT AND INSTINCTS

Even though it is wise to seek out the guidance of a financial planner, it's also crucial to understand the basics. A financial advisor will educate, advise, and assist you in taking action to develop a plan, but ultimately the final decisions are yours. A good financial planner will educate you about the options you face, acting as a teacher so you understand all the relevant issues. Then you can work together to create a plan and monitor it over the years. Following a successful financial plan is an ongoing process that enables you to stay up-to-date with your situation.

> A good financial planner will educate you about the options you face

People have vastly different opinions on most topics, whether it's religion, politics, stocks, insurance, sales loads, or how to finance your house. There are many individual considerations, and the correct solution depends on a variety of factors. We are leery of advice that suggests you should "always" do this or "never" do that. We believe most financial decisions are far grayer than they are black and white.

With the above in mind, if there is a decision or a direction you definitely should (or should not) take, we will tell you. For those decisions that are not so obvious, we will educate you and help you understand the options so you can make an informed decision. Our clients tell us, "That's exactly how I work with my patients."

We are not the first to say this, and we certainly won't be the last: "It is crucial to trust your own judgment and instincts before taking action, no matter how good an argument someone makes." The best way to gain confidence in your own better judgment is to educate yourself on the topic at hand.

In this book, you'll find answers to the most important financial questions everyone faces:

- How much money should I have in emergency reserves?
- In which order should I go about paying off my debts?
- Which is the right kind of insurance for me, and how much do I need?
- What are the most common financial mistakes people make?
- What types of retirement or investment accounts should I be using?

2

WHERE DO I START?

Three key elements that help you see where you stand financially are your net worth, your credit score, and a budget. Let's look at each one in detail.

YOUR NET WORTH

The starting point of any financial plan is to figure out your current net worth—a snapshot of what you are worth at an exact point in time. To determine your net worth, simply add up all your assets and subtract all your liabilities (debts). Often, when you are finishing your residency or fellowship training, your net worth is actually a negative number because the liabilities exceed the assets.

To measure your financial progress, it is important to know your net worth. Many people measure their financial progress by how much money they have in the bank. In reality, as the value of your assets goes up, such as a house, business, or investments, and as you pay debts down, your net worth might be increasing more dramatically than you think. The most important way to measure financial progress is to calculate your net worth regularly. We do this to monitor your progress and spot trends, just like you would watch patients' cholesterol, blood pressure, or some other method of monitoring their health.

In simple terms, what would you be worth if you sold everything you owned, turned it into cash, and then paid off all your debts? If this is the first time you're preparing a net-worth statement, it's also a good idea to estimate what you think your net worth has been over the past few years. Hopefully, you will be pleasantly surprised at the progress you've made and the trajectory you are on.

There are several categories within the net-worth statement.

1. **Fixed assets**—Fixed assets are those assets that have a relatively low risk of a loss of principal or are backed by the government's or a financial institution's claims-paying ability. Don't confuse this with fixed-income investments (bonds); those belong in the variable assets category. Fixed assets include the most

conservative assets you have. A few examples include checking and savings accounts, money market funds, certificates of deposit, T-bills, EE savings bonds, and whole life insurance cash values. These are assets you have access to in an emergency; they are available any time, which means they are "liquid."

2. **Variable assets**—These include most other financial assets. Examples include stocks, bonds, mutual funds, real estate investment trusts, retirement plans, or any investment whose principal can fluctuate.

Your personal and other assets include tangible assets such as your house, personal or business property, vehicles, computers, and cameras.

Don't get too bogged down trying to establish a value for every piece of personal property. You might already have that information available from your homeowner's or renter's insurance policies, but if not, a rough estimate will work just fine. The main reason for gathering this information is to have an estimate so you can monitor trends.

Here is a planning tip that can save you a lot of time and effort in the event of a loss. Videotape a walkthrough of each room in your house, including closets and the garage. In the event of a loss, that will make it easy to document your assets for the insurance company's reporting purposes.

Let's look at an example of a net-worth statement. Here is a very basic net-worth statement for a young physician:

SAMPLE NET-WORTH STATEMENT

Assets	
Fixed Assets:	
Savings Account	$5,000
Checking Account	$3,000
Certificate of Deposit	$2,000
Total Fixed Assets	**$10,000**
Variable Assets:	
IRA	$3,000
Mutual Funds	$7,000
Individual Stocks	$2,000
Variable Life Cash Value	$2,000
403(b) Balance	$20,000
Total Variable Assets	**$34,000**
Personal and Other Assets:	
Condo	$200,000
Vehicle	$20,000
Personal Property	$20,000
Total Personal and Other	**$240,000**
Total Assets:	**$284,000**

Liabilities	
Mortgage	$190,000
Home Equity Line of Credit	$5,000
Vehicle Loan	$10,000
Student Loans	$140,000
Total Liabilities:	**$345,000**
Net Worth: Assets Minus Liabilities	**-$61,000**

By keeping a statement like this up-to-date, when you are reviewing your net worth after some time, you will be able to track how this category has changed or to account for money you have spent.

For your liabilities, list the amount you owe if you could pay off the amount today, not the total of the payments over time, which would include interest. Subtract your total liabilities from your assets to arrive at your net worth. If you're like many people, this can be a sobering experience. Don't forget to include all loans: mortgages, auto loans, credit cards, student loans, personal debts, and consumer debt.

Don't feel too upset if you learn that your net worth is negative. It is very common for young physicians to have negative net worth because of their student loans. However, remember that your education is an asset, and student loans are an investment in your financial future.

If you fit into the negative net-worth category, your first financial goal is to get your net worth back to zero. If that is the case, it is especially important to establish a financial plan and get control of your financial life as soon as possible. But instead of dreading the process, have some fun with it. Celebrate and congratulate yourself when you become "worthless," especially when you have worked hard to save, pay off debt, and get on top of your finances.

Ignore the urge to put your head in the sand and think you have no power over the situation.

You are not alone, and there's no reason to be embarrassed. To prove it, take a look at our government. Its high federal deficit sets a dangerous precedent, not only for our culture but also for the world's economy. No matter how big your debt problem, it looks relatively small in this light!

> Make up your mind now to reverse the situation.

Simply make up your mind now to reverse the situation, and be proud that you're taking the right steps. The obvious way to improve your net worth is to decrease your spending and/or increase your income and investments. Begin by taking a serious look at your spending habits and make sure you are doing everything you can to achieve first a zero, and eventually a positive net worth. Getting yourself back to financial stability might feel like a long and lonely road, but with the help of a financial planner (or at least by reading this book), you don't have to feel like you're doing it alone.

> In summary, the most critical starting point to a financial plan is evaluating your net worth.

Then, on a periodic basis, compare the results to establish trends and measure improvement. A convenient time to do this is once a year, when you're doing your taxes. This way, all the paperwork is readily available, and you're focused on your annual earnings and expenditures. Keep all the financial records together from each year's tax forms and net-worth calculations for easy reference.

YOUR BUDGET

After calculating your net worth, you'll want to look at your monthly budget and define exactly where your money is being spent. The categories of the monthly budget should also include any deductions from your paycheck like state and federal income taxes, Social Security, and employee benefits. Once you know your take-home pay, deduct all the fixed expenses and the estimated variable expenses.

Are you unable to account for where a large portion of your money goes? This is the case for many people. To overcome this, try the following tips:

- **Keep track of your spending for three months.** Record every cent you spend, whether it's for a candy bar, a cup of coffee, or your mortgage and car payment. Then tally these amounts and categorize them at the end of each month (some software programs, like Quicken, make this very easy) to see exactly where your paychecks are going.

- **Vow to go back to the days of *cash-only* transactions.** For everything other than your large monthly payments (and even those, if you want to get really serious), stop using your debit and credit cards or writing checks for day-to-day expenditures like groceries, drugstore items, and clothing. It feels much different when you have to shell out $50 cash for a purchase than to hand over a piece of plastic.

- **Treat your savings account or investment amount like a bill you pay every month, like any other.** Experience has shown that if you don't get in the habit of saving money on a regular basis, either through a payroll deduction or an automatic withdrawal from your checking account, the money you intended to go toward savings or investments is mysteriously spent elsewhere.

How quickly you can move toward financial security depends on how motivated you are to save money.

It's not easy for Americans to live on less than their income, considering our credit-loving culture. However, if you start early enough, saving 15 percent of your gross income will typically be enough to help keep you safe from financial worries later on. If you are getting a later start, then you might need to live on 75 to 80 percent of your income and save 20 to 25 percent.

Saving or investing 15 percent of your income means you can live on 85 percent of your income. As elementary as this might sound, the significance is critical. In later years, these savings could accumulate to a substantial sum if invested properly. Also, it will teach you how to live below your means—a financial goal that seemingly every expert agrees on, but few physicians live by.

YOUR CREDIT SCORE

Most physicians do not look at a high credit score as an asset. We think this is a mistake. An important long-term financial strategy should be to monitor your credit score regularly and make decisions that strengthen and improve it. While in practice, continue to use credit, no matter how positive your cash flow is. Some physicians are in a fortunate position that they never need to take out a loan again or use a credit card. Avoid this cash-flow trap because it might come back to haunt you if/when if you apply for a mortgage on a second home, have a practice purchase/expansion, and/or cosign a loan for someone.

The importance of credit and the significance of monitoring your credit score on a consistent basis cannot be understated. The financial information included in your credit report will be a huge factor in whether you can obtain a loan, get auto or home insurance, rent an apartment, or even apply for a job. Also, your credit score is often the

most important factor in determining the interest rate at which you can obtain loans. The higher your score, the better off you will be. A higher score can save you tens of thousands of dollars in interest through the duration of a loan.

As a starting point, we suggest developing the habit of monitoring your credit score. It's a good idea to review your credit report at least once per year. Start at www.annualcreditreport.com or www.creditkarma.com. If you find any errors, contact the credit bureaus to correct them immediately. We recommend these frequent checks to monitor identity-theft issues and accidentally missed payments that can have catastrophic effects on your credit score. The three credit bureaus—Equifax, Experian, and TransUnion—all allow you to pull your credit report for free once per year. Each of these bureaus can contain a little different information, and they calculate your scores in slightly different ways.

It is helpful to know how your credit score is calculated. Knowing what types of activity contribute to the score, and to what degree, can help you prioritize financial activity and decision making as you take a proactive approach to improving and increasing your personal score. Here is the breakdown:[1]

- **Payment history: 35 percent**—More than one-third of the score is developed from your *payment history*. You are penalized by payments occurring later than thirty days past the due date. The later you are, the more detrimental the effect on your score.

- **Amounts owed: 30 percent**—Not quite one-third of your score is derived from the amount of money you owe, or your *credit utilization*. Ideally, the credit bureaus would like to see approximately 20 to 30 percent in use, with the first mark against you being made at 50 percent. This is the ratio of debt in use to debt available. This is on a per card/account basis. For example, if you have a credit card with a $3,000 limit, you want to keep a balance of less than $1,000 (33 percent)

---

1. "What's in My FICO® Scores?" Fair Isaac Corporation, https://www. myfico.com/credit-education/whats-in-your-credit-score.

17

per month on that card, and certainly no more than $1,500 (50 percent) per month.

- **Length of credit history: 15 percent**—Another 15 percent of the final score comes from your *credit history*. This is how long you have had credit. Positive credit payment history stays on your score for ten years, and negative history, as well as a positive payment on collection issues, stays on your report for seven years. (Keep longstanding accounts open, even if you no longer use them. Closing them can hurt your score.)

- **Credit mix: 10 percent**—Ten percent of your score comes from the *types of credit used*—installment, revolving, etc. Try to keep a mix of different types of credit.

- **New credit: 10 percent**—The final 10 percent of your score comes *new credit*. Research shows that opening several credit accounts in a short period of time represents a greater risk— especially for people who don't have a long credit history. If you can avoid it, try not to open too many accounts too rapidly.

> One planning tip we recommend is, in an effort to maintain and keep (or raise) your credit score, finance at least a portion of a car loan, even if you have the cash to pay for the vehicle outright. Then pay it off completely after making thirteen monthly payments. Or take out a small loan (only if terms are favorable) or a credit card jointly with your college-age child. This will help him or her establish credit, utilization, and payment history. Plus, your adult children might thank you when they buy their first home or get their first vehicle loan out of college because of their higher credit scores. Financially independent kids are a good investment!

3

THE PYRAMID

If you dump all the pieces of a puzzle on a table, it is initially a daunting task to begin putting the puzzle together. Where do you start? If you take one puzzle piece out of the pile at random, it's hard to know where that piece fits into the big picture. It is much easier to put the puzzle together if you have a picture of what the scene will look like once it's completed. So you look at the picture on the box to give you a guide to what the puzzle looks like when completed.

Similarly, we designed the financial pyramid as a method of seeing how a properly designed financial plan looks when it is put together correctly.

FOUR MAIN STAGES OF FINANCIAL PLANNING

As you can see in the diagram that follows, there are four main stages to the financial planning pyramid: The Security and Confidence Stage, The Capital Accumulation Stage, The Tax-Advantaged Stage, and The Speculation Stage.

The financial pyramid is a method of explaining the financial planning concept by categorizing your financial plan into stages. Of course, individual goals, habits, accomplishments, and so on are all unique, but most people share the same fundamental life stages. As a method of simply and efficiently organizing your financial life, the pyramid represents the keys to financial independence and demonstrates the basic goal of increasing your assets and reducing your debt so you can have enough money invested to retire comfortably. One individual might place more or less importance on one section of the pyramid than another, which is perfectly acceptable.

PYRAMID OF FINANCIAL NEEDS

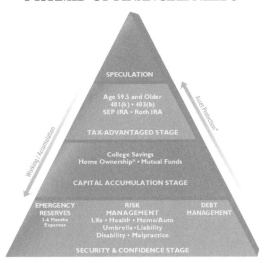

Financial advisors do not provide mortgage, tax, or legal advice, and this should not be considered as such. Please consult a mortgage, tax, or legal professional for advice regarding your specific mortgage, tax, or legal situation.

BALANCE THE FOUR STAGES OVER YOUR LIFETIME

Without a doubt, organizing your finances in an effort to build a solid base is the first step. If you don't do this, you may be subjecting your financial situation to undue risk, which will cause problems later on. On the other hand, it's also important not to place too much emphasis on only one stage, neglecting the overall balance. This could be a sign of being overly conservative. As an example, not taking advantage of higher-potential returns in equity (stock) investments might mean losing your purchasing power in the long run. The dollars might be worth less due to the effects of taxes and inflation.

It is very important to try to accomplish a lifelong financial balance.

You certainly don't want to get to retirement age with a huge amount of money saved up, only to be in poor health and not be able to enjoy it. That's true especially if you scrimped and saved your whole life, working so hard that you didn't enjoy yourself along the way. By the same token, you don't want to near retirement and realize you haven't saved enough and now must take a substantial drop in your standard of living or go back to working just to survive. The ideal situation is to retire at the same or a greater standard of living than that you were accustomed to in your working years, but not feel at any time that you have greatly sacrificed.

LIVE ON LESS THAN YOUR INCOME

A fundamental of short- and long-term financial success is living on less than your income. If you can get used to living on 80 to 85 percent of your income, this allows you to commit 15 to 20 percent of your income to your net worth. Initially, this might mean aggressively paying off loans, but over time, you should save the majority of this extra income. If you are living paycheck to paycheck, is there a way you can decrease your expenses and/or increase your income so you can start building some surplus funds into your monthly budget?

KEEP ALL YOUR "PLATES" SPINNING

The ideal investment is completely liquid and has many tax advantages, a great rate of return, and low risk. If you find an advisor or salesman claiming to have such an investment, you would be wise to avoid that person. This ideal investment does not exist!

Let's use an analogy of spinning plates. If you have ever been to a circus or seen a juggler, you may have seen the performer attempt to spin a lot of plates on long sticks...all at the same time. The objective is to allocate limited energy in such a manner that enables you to keep all the plates spinning. It doesn't do any good to devote a lot of time to one spinning plate while the others are slowing down, wobbling, and falling down. The goal is to keep all the plates spinning!

Your financial plan is on somewhat the same level, with each financial decision representing a different plate. First of all, you need to find out which plates you want to start spinning and then direct your dollars to keep them going. You could have several debt-reduction plates, some risk-management (insurance) plates, retirement and/or college education plates, and so on. Each individual's situation is going to be different. Again, there are limited resources that need to be allocated in a way that enables you to accomplish all your goals. This is where the advice of a professional and experienced financial advisor can be valuable.

THE HIGHER THE STAGE, THE LESS LIQUID THE FUNDS

The key financial variables in the pyramid are risk, liquidity, rate of return, and tax advantages. The money in your emergency reserves and at the Security and Confidence Stage should be very liquid or accessible. Generally, as you move to higher stages in the pyramid, the less liquid your funds become.

> The key financial variables are risk, liquidity, rate of return, and tax advantages.

Risk and rate of return tend to go hand in hand. The higher the amount of risk you take, the higher the rate of return potential should be… given time. In the pyramid, typically lower risk with lower rates of return should be at the base of your planning, and the risk and rate of return increase as you move up the pyramid. Historically, stock market and investing returns have less volatility the longer the time frame that is considered. Keep in mind, however, that past performance is not indicative of future results.

TAX ADVANTAGES ARE AT THE HIGHER STAGES

From a tax standpoint, there are typically not too many tax advantages at the lower level. If you have money in a savings account, that money is generating ordinary income, and you are paying tax on it, so there are no tax advantages there. On the other hand, when you put money into a qualified retirement plan, the contribution is on a before-tax basis, so the tax is delayed and deferred to a later date. Under most circumstances, however, you cannot touch the money in your qualified plan until age 59½ without paying a 10 percent early-withdrawal penalty, plus the income taxes due on that amount.

The rule of thumb on tax savings is similar to risk and rate of return. As you move up the pyramid, you'll have greater potential for tax advantages on your investments.

4

THE SECURITY AND CONFIDENCE STAGE

As you begin building a well-structured, sound financial plan, your first priorities need to be centered on three key issues. These issues represent the building blocks for your entire plan going forward. Regardless of what stage of financial planning you are in, it is critical that you do the following:

- Build and maintain adequate emergency-fund cash reserves.
- Have debt under control and a structured system for repayment.
- Secure appropriate insurance protection.

While the details of each of these steps will vary significantly depending on the person, all sound financial plans have these three components in order. Each of these factors is equally important. Most people agree on the need to have money accessible for emergencies, to pay their debts (especially on high-interest credit cards), and to be adequately insured. The trick to the individual financial plan is to figure out the appropriate amount for each of these.

1. EMERGENCY RESERVES

Does your financial agenda resemble that of Will Rogers? He said, "I'm not so much concerned about the rate of return on my money, just the return of it."

During your residency training, your primary *financial* objectives are to:

- Keep your debt under control as much as possible.
- Try to live within (not beyond) your income.
- Develop good financial-planning habits.
- Educate yourself.

Perhaps the best habit to form that will continuously add value to your lifelong financial plan is keeping an adequate liquid-cash emergency-fund reserve. Regardless of where you are in your financial life, we advocate always maintaining an emergency-fund reserve. Generally, a good rule of thumb is to add all your total *fixed* monthly expenses and multiply that amount by 4 or 5.

In the absence of any large, anticipated purchases or expenses within the next twelve to twenty-four months, this is an adequate amount to hold in cash as an emergency-fund reserve. On a resident physician's salary, this is easier said than done! However, regardless of how tight your monthly budget is, we still advocate *paying yourself first* and contributing a fixed amount to a money market account every month. We recommend this even if the interest earned on a money market account is less than the interest being charged on a credit card or student-loan debt.

When you do this, you will accomplish two very important things. First, you can pay for unexpected expenses that continuously happen at the worst time without charging the entire bill on a credit card. Second, you develop the habit of systematically saving a portion of your income every month. This is a habit that will be of great value for the rest of your life. It will be far easier to incrementally increase savings as your income increases than it will to be forced to increase your savings later in life.

> Develop the habit of systematically saving a portion of your income every month.

Maintaining an adequate liquid-cash reserve is just as important for the well-established, high-income medical specialist; the reasons are just a bit different.

Emergency-Fund Reserves and Their Influence on Long-Term Rates of Return

A money market fund is essentially a mutual fund that you invest in short-term monetary instruments. It provides a relatively stable vehicle for your assets and generally offers higher return potential than a savings account.

Also, money market funds often have check-writing privileges. They are a low-risk investment that provides liquidity. The trade-off for such liquidity and general stability of principal is, of course, a very low rate of return. While money market funds have the benefit of stability, it's important to point out that they do have a slight degree of market risk. For the physician with a significant net worth, a high income, and a high level of financial security, the low return on a money market fund isn't very appealing and often leads to inadequate emergency-fund reserves. When the unexpected expense arises, other assets with greater degrees of price fluctuation must be tapped. Should you liquidate these other, more volatile assets at an inopportune time, the consequences can be devastating.

Consider the following example:

If you invested $10,000 over a fifteen-year period ending December 31, 2017, in a hypothetical investment that performed similarly to the unmanaged S&P 500, you would have experienced the following results:

- Fully invested for entire period $ 41,333
- Missed the best ten days $ 20,873
- Missed the best twenty days $ 13,629
- Missed the best thirty days $ 9,374
- Missed the best forty days $ 6,716

Results based on S&P 500 composite index without reinvested dividends. Past performance is not indicative of future results. You cannot invest directly in an index. Indices do not have expenses, and if they did, performance would be significantly lower. Figures assume the reinvestment of income and do not include transaction costs, taxes, or expenses. The chart represents past performance of the Standard and Poor's 500®, an unmanaged broad equity index. Large company stocks do not carry any guarantees. Investments in large company stocks will fluctuate and, when redeemed, may be worth more or less than originally contributed.

> Withdrawing investments originally intended for longer periods at a bad time can have a huge impact on your rate of return.

Just a few days "out of the market" can essentially ruin a perfectly prudent, well-structured, and properly allocated investment portfolio's rate of return. Adequate liquid-cash reserves will allow longer-term investments to remain just that: long-term investments!

The one constant in life is that there will always be surprises. The purpose of an emergency reserve fund is just what it sounds like—money that is very accessible when you really need it. The main characteristic of an investment in this category is that the money is liquid yet invested in more stable vehicles so the principal remains intact.

The most common mistake people make here is not having adequate reserves or taking undue risk with these funds. This money needs to remain liquid in case of unexpected expenses like car repairs, home repairs, job loss, or medical emergencies. For most people, the main benefit of having an adequate emergency reserve fund is having access to funds when they need them. When you are financially prepared for these surprises, they become less stressful and are therefore easier to deal with emotionally. Furthermore, when there is a source of funds for these types of emergencies, you do not have to rely on credit cards or personal, unsecured, high-interest loans.

A money market mutual fund is often the best choice for your emergency reserves. Many people incorrectly associate the term "mutual fund" with high risk. However, a mutual fund has only as much risk as its underlying investments. A money market mutual fund pools investors' dollars in the typical mutual-fund style and purchases through banks, treasury securities (T bills), and commercial paper.

> Most money-market funds offer a check-writing privilege, which allows you to write checks against your account, subject to minimums of usually $250 or $500. The rate of return earned on these funds will fluctuate based on the short-term money market but is typically competitive with the interest rate at the time.

Investments in a money market fund are neither insured nor guaranteed by the FDIC or any government agency. Although the fund seeks to preserve the value of your investment at $1 per share, it is possible to lose money by investing in the fund. Money market funds may also impose a fee upon sale of your shares or may temporarily suspend your ability to sell shares if the fund's liquidity falls below required minimums because of market conditions or other factors.

Life insurance cash values on permanent policies (i.e., whole life, adjustable life, universal life) can also be important sources of emergency reserve funds. These funds typically earn a competitive fixed rate of return, and they are accessible. It is usually possible to take out a loan or borrow against your cash value, using it as collateral; sometimes you can take an outright withdrawal of this money. Remember, though, that any loans or withdrawals you take will reduce both your policy's cash value and your death benefit, and they might be restricted in the first several years of the contract. Also, please remember that the primary reason to purchase a life insurance policy is the death benefit. We discuss this topic thoroughly in chapter 6.

A home equity line of credit is another option. With equity in your house, and with interest rates low and tax-deductible, this option is worth considering. In fact, during times when interest rates are low, maintaining an open line of credit against your home equity can be a viable source of emergency-reserve cash. You can also use your equity to pay down a high-interest credit card or for a major purchase like a car. The drawback is that it needs to be paid off when you sell your house, which of course would result in less proceeds at closing.

> If your house were to decline in value, creating less equity, you might have to pay off the home equity line and/or face a higher interest rate on the loan.

While interest rates on home-equity loans are higher than a few years ago, this might still be an option worth considering, especially if you can use the money to pay off higher-interest consumer debt. Please note that the terms of arrangements for a home-equity line of credit are controlled by the lending institution, and you should review them with your legal advisor.

2. DEBT MANAGEMENT AND STUDENT LOANS

If you are in the fortunate situation of having no debts, congratulations! If you come from the school of thought that you don't ever want to owe anything to anybody, debt management is not an issue. However, in today's society, this ideology is very uncommon. Many people could use some strategies on effectively managing their debt.

Financially, it makes sense to rank all your debts, from highest to lowest interest, paying attention to the after-tax cost of borrowing. Because consumer debt is not tax-deductible, those rates are taken at face value. However, a mortgage or home-equity loan *is* deductible, so the real rate of return is the after-tax cost.

Another general rule of thumb is that you should pay off credit cards and consumer debt first if they have the highest interest rates.

Then you would want to work away at the furniture loan, the used-car loan, the new-car loan, student loans, and finally the home mortgage. Nowadays, many credit cards offer very low interest rates on balance transfers, which can be a temporary solution. But make sure the rate after the introductory period is not higher than the rate on your current card.

It is also important to look at debt management from a cash-flow standpoint, as well as an emotional standpoint. With this in mind, it can make sense to pay off a lower-interest loan if it will improve your cash flow dramatically, or if emotionally it is important for you to get it paid off for some other reason. Many people find a sense of satisfaction in paying debts off completely. Once one debt is paid off, take any extra cash and immediately begin paying off another loan more aggressively so that cash does not get absorbed into your budget.

If you are still in your training years, you should also look into income-driven repayment options that allow you to make payments that are relative to your income. For the most up-to-date details, visit studentaid.ed.gov/sa.

Student Loans

Quite possibly, the topic that younger physicians ask us about most often is student loans. With varying interest rates, multiple loan servicers, potential forgiveness programs, and balances into the six figures, it's no wonder there are so many questions. Fortunately, from an analysis perspective, there are really two trains of thought when it comes to student-loan repayment: either try to qualify for loan forgiveness, or refinance your loans to secure the lowest interest rate possible.

Public Service Loan Forgiveness Program (PSLFP)

The concept of this program is simple enough, yet the outlook isn't black and white. This government program was introduced in 2007. The government wanted to find a way to help alleviate the debt crisis many young professionals in America face. So they created the Public Service Loan Forgiveness Program. In summary, this program is designed for people working in government or nonprofit entities. Those who work full time (more than thirty hours per week) for a qualifying program, while paying their loans on time under one of the appropriate repayment programs, will have the balance of their loans forgiven after 120 payments (ten years of monthly payments).

> Most academic and community hospitals qualify as
> nonprofit hospitals and are therefore
> eligible for this program, which is great news
> for residents and fellows.

Eligible Repayment Strategies

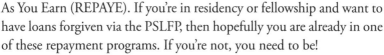

To qualify for the PSLFP, you need to be paying off your loans in one of four ways: with Ten-Year Standard Repayment, Income-Based Repayment (IBR), Pay As You Earn (PAYE), or Revised Pay As You Earn (REPAYE). If you're in residency or fellowship and want to have loans forgiven via the PSLFP, then hopefully you are already in one of these repayment programs. If you're not, you need to be!

This program allows you to log as many low payments as you can on your race to 120 total payments, which should maximize the amount forgiven in the end. Below is a description of each qualifying payment route:

- **Ten-year standard**—Obviously, this is not the solution because the day you would be eligible for any forgiveness would also be the day you finish paying off your loans!

- **IBR**—This is generally 15 percent (10 percent if you took your loans out after 2014) of your discretionary income, regardless of your student-loan balance. The total amount owed will never be higher than the ten-year standard amount.

- **PAYE**—This is generally 10 percent of your discretionary income, regardless of your student-loan balance. The total amount owed will never be higher than the ten-year standard amount. Typically, this is a better option than IBR because the monthly obligation is about 30 percent lower. However, not everyone qualifies for this program.

- **REPAYE**—The Obama administration introduced this program in December 2015. As the name alludes to, the intent of this program was to revise the rules surrounding PAYE to allow everyone to be eligible for the 10 percent obligation (as opposed to the 15 percent IBR amount). Essentially, it's the same as PAYE but with three major differences—two cons and one massive pro.

   1. One "con" is that with REPAYE, both spouses' incomes count to factor in how much you owe per month. Many doctors are married but file taxes separately to keep their income lower and their monthly loan obligation lower. In REPAYE, that strategy no longer exists; both spouses' incomes count, regardless of how you file taxes.

   2. The other major flaw is that there is no cap in the amount you will owe per month in REPAYE. This is different than both IBR and PAYE, where the most you'll owe

on a monthly basis is whatever the ten-year standard repayment amount is. If you have a high-income specialty or a high-income-earning spouse, this is a significant flaw. With no cap in the amount you owe per month, there's a good chance you will file a number of years with very high payments and therefore have little to nothing forgiven at the end of your 120 payments.

3. The major positive factor—and this cannot be understated for resident/fellow physicians—is the *interest subsidy* offered via REPAYE. If your monthly obligation does not meet the interest you owe on a monthly basis (which is common for residents/fellows), then the government will pick up the tab on the additional interest you owe on all subsidized loans for three years (this is also true in IBR and PAYE) *and* 50 percent of the interest on unsubsidized loans. (This is not the case with IBR or PAYE.) In some cases, you could save thousands of dollars. Therefore, we recommend that you give REPAYE strong consideration, at least for the short term, while you are in training.

The information provided here is current as of 2018. You can find more information about these loan-repayment programs at https:// studentaid.ed.gov/sa/.

Public Service Loan Forgiveness Outlook

As of the writing of this book, *nobody* has had their loans forgiven from this program—not because it will never happen, but because we haven't reached the ten-year mark yet. None of us has a crystal ball to tell us what this program will look like five or more years from now, but we haven't met a ton of people optimistic about its long-term success. Our guess is that over time, this program will evolve and include some kind of a tax, a limit, or an income threshold to make people eligible for forgiveness.

Given our current government deficit, it's easy to imagine those in the administration changing their minds about the massive amounts of loans they are forgiving. This is what scares us about this program's long-term outlook. However, because these options don't currently exist, we don't discourage people from pursuing them; we just want you to be conscious of the reality of the logistics behind this program. If you are a good candidate for it, you should file the Public Service Employment Certification Form annually. You can access it at https://studentaid.ed.gov/sa/ by typing "employment certification form" in the search box.

Privately Refinancing Your Loans

If you read the first half of this chapter and think the PSLFP is not the best option for you (either because you are/will be working in private practice, want to pay off your debt aggressively, or simply don't believe in the outlook of the program), then there is another route to consider: privately refinancing your loans to secure a lower interest rate. By not pursuing PSLFP, you are conceding that you will need to pay off the entirety of your loans, and like any debt, you want to pay as little in interest as possible along the way.

> Refinancing your loans can secure a drastically lower interest rate, and you can even do so while in residency or fellowship.

Currently, a number of banks are willing to refinance student loans for physicians. A simple Google search will reveal numerous potential suitors for you to review. The concept is incredibly simple: a bank pays off your loan balance (the principal and that pesky high interest). In return, you owe the bank the same amount, but at a lower interest rate. If you have $200,000 worth of loans at 6.8 percent, you might be able to refinance those loans at maybe 4.8 percent. That's essentially $4,000 per year in interest that you would no longer have to pay! The simple act of refinancing could create a massive swing in your overall repayment total.

With most banks, when you refinance, you instantly jump into the full repayment amount. This is important because if you're in residency or fellowship, that monthly obligation is likely not feasible. Fortunately, there are at least three financial institutions willing to offer residents or fellows low refinancing rates, and they will defer the majority of the payment until your training program has concluded. As of the writing of this book, Laurel Road, SoFi, and Link Capital offer special "training" programs for residents and fellows, although we anticipate this landscape to change. Consult with a financial professional to discuss additional options.

> The thing to be cautious about when looking to lower your interest rate is that you concede all government benefits when you refinance.

There will be no more forgiveness or ability to go into forbearance, and in some cases, the obligation is still due if you die (though most companies have waived this now). Consider these changes before you look to refinance.

In summary, if you have a long training program or a large loan balance, then PSLFP might make sense for you. However, if you're in a short training program, got a late start on repaying your loans, aren't optimistic about the program, or are one of the many people who just isn't a good candidate for loan forgiveness, then there's a good chance refinancing is the most efficient financial move. Carefully consider all your options, and work with a financial consultant who thoroughly knows the government repayment strategies and the refinancing opportunities that exist for physicians.

3. RISK MANAGEMENT

Protecting yourself against unforeseen catastrophic losses is the third critical area of the base of the pyramid and the *Security and Confidence Stage*. We call this protection "risk management." In fact, think of this as a three-legged stool: kick one leg out, and the stool will not stand. The financial pyramid is just like that.

Important insurance coverage can include health and major medical, auto, disability, long-term care, and homeowner's or renter's insurance. In many cases, life and/or disability insurance are overlooked. However,

these can be very important, depending on your personal situation.

The reason for placing risk management at this point is obvious: you need to protect yourself from losses that would create a hole so big that you might never be able to dig yourself out otherwise. Then, once you are on your way to financial independence, insurance plays an equally important role in protecting your assets.

While you don't want to have any gaps in your insurance protection, you certainly don't want to overlap or duplicate coverage. The ideal financial plan will have you paying reasonable premium levels while providing maximum protection. Remember, the major role of insurance is to protect against catastrophic losses. Common mistakes are trying to insure too many contingencies or not using deductibles to your advantage.

Ask yourself a couple of questions before you purchase insurance:

- Is the premium for this coverage going to dramatically affect my lifestyle?
- If I do not buy this coverage and suffer the losses that would have been covered, would I be in grave financial trouble?

If the answer to the first question is *no* and to the second *yes*, then the insurance in question is right for you. If not, reconsider the structure and price of the insurance. Consult an experienced financial professional to help you determine the appropriate levels of coverage and how to structure your insurance within the context of a comprehensive financial plan. We also believe life and disability insurance are so important for the physician that we are devoting the next two chapters to these topics.

Looking back to the Middle Ages, we get a glimpse of the importance of insurance. People of wealth built fabulous castles and filled them with treasures. They always devoted significant resources to protecting those assets in the form of an army, a moat, and so on. In a sense, that was an early form

> A moat, in a sense, was an early form of an insurance policy.

of an insurance policy. So, as you continue to build your net worth, review and update your insurance to be sure you are maximizing your coverage and protecting yourself, your family, and your wealth.

For starters, we recommend making sure you have the basics covered— health insurance, auto insurance, and renter's/homeowner's insurance. This will serve as the base level to your risk-management corner of the pyramid before you acquire other types of coverage.

Umbrella Liability Coverage

If you are ever sued, your standard homeowner's or auto policy will provide you with *some* liability coverage. It will pay for judgments against you and your attorney's fees, up to the limit set in the policy. But if you want to have an extra layer of liability protection, that is what an umbrella policy provides.

> Generally speaking, an umbrella policy kicks in when you reach the limit on the underlying liability coverage in a homeowner's, renter's, condo, or auto policy. It should also cover you for libel and slander. Please note that coverage might vary for your specific policy.

Because the personal umbrella policy goes into effect after the underlying coverage is exhausted, there are certain limits that usually must be met to purchase this coverage. Most insurers will want you to have a minimum of $250,000 of liability insurance on your auto policy and $300,000 of liability insurance on your homeowner's policy before they will sell you umbrella liability in the amount of $1 million of additional coverage.

This amount varies by carrier; however. For about $200 per year, you can buy a $1 million policy. The policy can be increased in million-dollar increments. Generally speaking, umbrella liability coverage is cheapest when you combine it with your homeowner's, renter's, and auto insurance.

Identity Theft[2]

We are all vulnerable. According to www.ftc.gov, identity theft has been the number one consumer complaint to the Federal Trade Commission for the past fifteen years straight. This crime affects millions of Americans each year and costs billions of dollars and significant time as victims struggle to put their lives back together. Take steps now to reduce your risk, and have seasoned professionals help you if you are victimized.

Their professional services should include the following:

- **Privacy and security monitoring of your personal information.** Credit/financial fraud is the number one reported type of identity theft. However, credit-report monitoring alone is not enough. By the end of 2017, medical identity theft had increased by 40 percent from the previous year and is growing rapidly, so it is also a key area to protect.[3]

- **Professional consultation whenever you need it, including**

---

2. Financial advisors do not provide identity-theft protection services. This section is for informational purposes only.

3. *Consumer Sentinel Network Data Book 2017*, Federal Trade Commission, March 2018.

24/7 emergency access to attorneys and licensed private in-vestigators. If a thief has committed a crime in your name, being able to call your attorney immediately can make the difference between being arrested and going to jail or going on your way. A private investigator can help minimize the damage of identity theft—and the stress.

- **Complete identity restoration done for you by licensed private investigators.** Expert thieves are stealing our information, and experts are needed to untangle identify-theft messes—whether they are related to medical, character/criminal, driver's license, Social Security number, financial, or other theft—so that you can get on with your life. It may give you confidence to have licensed investigators on standby, ready to go to work on your behalf and committed to working until your identity is back to where it was before the fraud occurred.

5

DISABILITY INCOME INSURANCE

Unless you are independently wealthy, your ability to earn an income is your greatest financial asset. Protecting this income should be a primary objective of every financial plan. Therefore, a thorough understanding of disability insurance and all its features is a fundamental objective of this book.

WHAT IS DISABILITY INSURANCE?

Disability insurance is insurance on your greatest financial asset: your income and your ability to earn that income in the future. This is an especially important insurance policy for the high-income specialist. Given the numbers of years you have spent on education and training, your skills are unique. If a sickness or accident occurs that renders you unable to perform these unique skills, disability insurance is what allows you to stay in your home, pay your bills, and continue to provide for your family's financial needs.

> A disability income policy must have features and benefits that match your unique skills and fulfill the intended purpose of replacing income in the event of disability.

Here is an explanation of the features and benefits you should consider.

HOW IS A DISABILITY DEFINED?

The definition of a disability is perhaps the most important feature of a policy. We suggest using a policy that has true "own occupation" specialty-specific coverage. If you are unable to practice your unique skills, the resulting loss of income is replaced. However, there are several different levels of "own occupation" coverage.

- **True own occupation**—A policy that has "true own occupation" coverage will pay the stated benefit of the disability policy if you cannot perform the exact duties of your occupation. The policy would continue to pay the full benefits of the contract, even if you were able to work and generate an income. If you are not working in your exact field, the policy pays. A neurosurgeon unable to practice neurosurgery due to an accident or sickness but who is able to work in an administrative position would receive the *full* disability benefit. Furthermore, if that same neurosurgeon started a business and eventually earns more than he or she was earning as a neurosurgeon, he or she would still receive the full benefits with a true own occupation disability plan.

> A policy with "true own occupation" coverage will typically be more expensive. However, such an "ironclad" definition of a disability is a very important feature to consider, especially with physicians who have sub-specialty training. The greater the amount of training and the more specialized you become, the greater your need for a "true own occupation" policy.

There are also policies with "transitional own occupation" coverage.

- **Transitional occupation**—A policy that has a "transitional own occupation" definition is a bit different than the above "true own occupation." If you cannot practice your duties due to an accident or sickness, a policy with this type of coverage would pay the stated benefit for as long as you are disabled. Your unique duties and skills are covered. The difference between the two policy definitions becomes evident if you retrain and return to work in another field. With a regular occupation definition, the disability benefits would begin to be reduced as income from another occupation increases. Should this income from another occupation exceed the income you generated as a medical specialist, the disability benefits would cease. Such a definition of disability will have a lower premium than the above "true own occupation."

FUTURE INSURABILITY OPTIONS

It is easy to see why disability insurance is an important element of a sound financial plan. However, a resident physician earning $50,000 per year with no other sources of income, a mortgage payment, a car payment, and a spouse at home with children might not have enough disposable income to purchase a large disability policy.

Thus, one of the more important disability policy features that any physician should consider is a "future purchase" or "future insurability" option. This feature allows the insured to increase the amount of disability coverage in the future, when income is higher, without having to prove medical insurability.

Let's look at an example of why this type of feature can have a real-life impact.

One of our young radiology residents had a wife who worked at home managing the household, and his salary at the time was about $50,000 per year. His situation was a bit unique for two reasons. First, he was very fortunate not to have any student loans. Second, he was able to supplement his income with regular moonlighting. Even with those two exceptions, however, their monthly cash flow was tight, and they were unwilling to consider disability insurance, viewing it as yet another expense they could do without. It was, in their minds, a simple question of priorities. Besides, he was young and healthy, and in just a

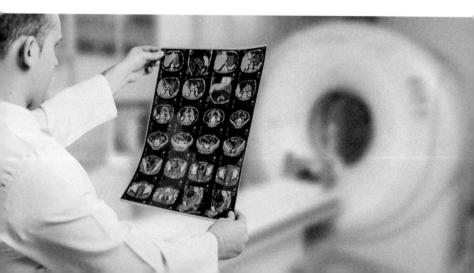

few short years, his income in private practice would be much higher. He figured he would worry about disability insurance at that time.

We were unable to convince them of the importance of protecting their future income.

Fast-forward three years to the end of his residency training. Upon completion of residency, he was offered his dream job in his and his wife's hometown of Detroit. They were both very excited to finally be done living check to check, be closer to family, and move on with the next phase of life. They had big plans as well, all of which were dependent on his income. There was one small hitch with the radiology group he joined, though: it did not offer group long-term disability. This meant he would be forced to cover his income entirely through individual disability insurance.

The thought of having no income protection, with so many plans they had made, was a risk they could not afford to take. An accident, sickness, or some ailment that would prevent him from practicing radiology could send many of their dreams up in smoke.

During the underwriting process, he learned he had adult-onset diabetes. This was the first he knew of his condition, and it meant, from a disability insurance standpoint, that he would be uninsurable forever. He and his wife determined that being unable to protect his income was too great a risk. So he took a different job with a different group that had a group long-term disability plan.

> It meant, from a disability insurance standpoint, that he would be uninsurable forever.

As a member of the group, he automatically received coverage under the group long-term disability plan. Even though the coverage amount was less than half his income, it was something. Although the job was still in Detroit, it was much farther away, with lower pay, and in a less-than-ideal environment for him.

The inability to protect his income could have been avoided had he purchased an individual disability policy with a future income protection rider that allowed him to increase his coverage when he entered private practice—*without* evidence of medical insurability.

> The inability to protect his income could have been avoided.

A medical specialist looking to protect his or her income but unwilling or unable to afford a large disability premium at the present time could purchase a disability policy that protects current income with a future purchase option or future insurability agreement (different companies have different names) that gives the insured the guaranteed ability to increase coverage in the future. Many companies will allow up to an additional $10,000 to $15,000 per month of benefit, no medical questions asked. The cost of this feature is either free or adds a minimal amount to the monthly premium. This is a very low cost to guarantee your ability to increase coverage in the future.

RESIDUAL/PARTIAL DISABILITY BENEFITS

Many disabilities are not total and complete. The residual disability benefit feature would pay a monthly benefit should you suffer a *partial* loss of income. There are very few, if any, group long-term disability plans that have such a feature. Under most group plans, you must be completely and totally disabled and under the constant care of a physician to receive a disability benefit.

For example, a radiologist who loses the use of her hand and is unable to perform interventional procedures but can still read film and perform many of the normal duties would qualify. If her interventional procedures were responsible for a significant portion of income, the loss of such income can still have a devastating effect on her financial life. Any individual disability policy should have a rider that would pay a percentage of income lost resulting from a partial disability.

NON-CANCELABLE/GUARANTEED RENEWABLE

We recommend disability policies that are non-cancelable and guaranteed renewable. This means that as long as you pay your premium on time, the company cannot cancel your coverage or raise your rates. Given the importance of disability coverage and knowing it will be a policy you own for many years, experiencing no change in your premium cost or coverage can provide real peace of mind and should always be a feature of your disability plan.

COST OF LIVING ADJUSTMENT

This particular feature becomes extremely beneficial for disabilities that are more long term. This feature protects the benefit's net purchasing power against inflation once you qualify for a claim. A common COLA on a physician's disability policy is 3 percent.

EXCLUSIONS

Ideally, insurance policies would not have loopholes, exclusions, or preexisting exclusion riders; coverage would be guaranteed under any and all circumstances. But this is not the case. When analyzing your disability insurance needs, you must consider your area of specialty, understand the exclusions that exist on the policy, and determine if they are acceptable.

If the policy has exclusions, will your income still be, under most circumstances, adequately covered? This is a difficult question and will vary greatly from one medical specialty to another.

> Our advice to our physician clients is to look at the exclusion and determine if it is reasonable, given their specialty.

If the policy has all the features and benefits necessary to adequately cover your income in your particular specialty, and the exclusion is highly unlikely to be an issue, the coverage is acceptable. If not, look at another company that might have a slightly inferior policy but does not have the same exclusion.

For example, many (not all) companies have a mental and nervous exclusion. Policies with such an exclusion would treat a disability related to depression or anxiety differently than a muscular or skeletal accident. If your disability is due to depression, many disability companies would pay a benefit only for a limited period of time, typically twenty-four months. After that, if you are still not working due to depression-related issues, the disability benefit would stop.

> It is very important to understand the exclusions, know when they may come into play, and determine if they are acceptable, given the other features and benefits of the contract.

CONCLUSION

Without a doubt, a correctly structured disability policy is a critical element in any physician's financial plan. Over the years, we have witnessed many examples of this. Uninsured, disabled physicians have let us know that they wish their advisors had been more adamant about them purchasing a policy, as we described.

Disabled physicians who are insured have been able to continue being paid, their children can remain in the same schools, life can go on, and they can direct all their energy and focus where it should be—dealing with the disability and recovery—not worrying about finances.

6

LIFE INSURANCE

The subject of life insurance is very confusing to many physicians because there are so many products, solutions, and opinions. Just a quick Google search will bring up thousands of articles, websites, and links. Unfortunately, this information is often biased or skewed in one way or another. In this chapter, we will attempt to educate you about this decision, simplify it, and provide you with a decision tree that you can use.

> A successful financial plan provides you with confidence, minimizes worry and stress, and offers options and choices to enhance your financial well-being.

As mentioned earlier, a successful financial plan provides financial strength and confidence and minimizes worry and stress. In addition, it offers options and choices to enhance and complement a comprehensive financial plan. Life insurance, as a properly structured component of a comprehensive plan, not only provides dollars to spouses, partners, children, and heirs, but depending on the type of policy, can also provide some of the following benefits:

- Protection for your insurability in the event of a health change
- Security for a job change without having to rely on group benefits for all your coverage
- A source of cash for emergencies and/or opportunities[4]
- A guarantee of the ability to convert to a permanent product as your cash flow allows[5]
- Allowance for continuation of coverage during a long-term disability if a waiver of premium for disability clause is added to the policy

---

4. Policy loans and withdrawals can create an adverse tax result in the event of a lapse or policy surrender and will reduce both the cash value and death benefit.

5. Terms and conditions vary by product and provider.

- The ability to use the cash value early, in the event of a long-term-care need[6]

- Tax-deferred growth of cash values and, if structured correctly (we'll address that later in this chapter), the ability to use them in a tax-favored manner

- Asset protection…in some states, the cash value is an exempt asset from claims of creditors.[7]

- Estate planning uses that can help you maximize the estate you leave to your heirs and to charities

- Security of a bank loan and/or buyout of a deceased partner in a business

HOW MUCH LIFE INSURANCE DO YOU NEED?

Please see the following graph for a visual depiction of a typical person's need for life insurance.

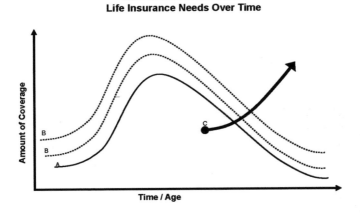

Life Insurance Basics
Life Insurance Needs Over Time

The solid line labeled "A" illustrates that at an early age, you might not need any (or not much) coverage. As you get older, you might be in a relationship, start a family, take on a mortgage, and/or buy into a practice, and your need for life insurance increases. How much coverage

---

6. This feature is generally available through an optional rider and is available for an additional fee; restrictions and limitations might apply.

7. Applicability might be subject to restrictions. Consult a local attorney.

you need and how long this need lasts depends on a lot of variables, and everyone is different. But there is an economic and emotional toll that your death may present, and life insurance is the most economical method of addressing this.

As you get older, typically your needs start to decrease. For example, as you pay off debts, you build other assets, and your children become self-sufficient (hopefully!). In fact, many people would look at this graph and conclude that they might not need any life insurance at they get older. Conceptually, this makes sense, especially for people who are debt-free and have built up a substantial asset base. However, the dotted lines (labeled "B") illustrate the fact that this line representing nsurance need goes up every year due to inflation.

The point labeled "C" triggers an interesting situation.

People who are very successful financially—and frankly, are financially independent and might not need life insurance for the original reasons—might want to keep (or buy new) coverage as a very effective method of paying estate taxes so that the estate they have built more efficiently transfers to heirs or charities.

Also, owning a life insurance policy at retirement can act as a "permission slip" to be more aggressive in living on the principal of your investments, knowing that the death benefit provided due to a premature death replaces those assets to your survivors, depending on those assets.

As for how much you might need, this is an interesting topic. Think about the following statements, and see if any of them apply to your thinking:

- "My partner (or spouse) has a good job and should be able to continue to work if I die, so I probably don't need much coverage."
- "I have all the coverage I need through work/my employer/ my group."
- "I'm a stay-at-home parent and do not bring in any income, so I do not need any life insurance."
- "I'm single right now and not in a relationship. Therefore, I don't have any dependents, so why would I consider life insurance at this point in my life?"
- "Why would I ever consider insuring my children?"
- "I have read that cash-value life insurance is a bad investment and that you should never combine the two."

We have heard all these comments and many more. Hopefully, the following discussion will help you understand this complicated product and decisions surrounding it.

THE IMPORTANCE OF "HUMAN LIFE VALUE"

The maximum you can buy is based on your "Human Life Value." Each insurance company uses different methods of calculating the maximum coverage that it is willing to offer, but the total usually comes to about twenty to thirty times your annual income. Essentially, this is the present value of your lifetime income stream. Ideally, if life insurance were free, we would all obtain this amount, wouldn't you agree?

Because it is not free, and because most people are juggling many competing goals with their finances, a decision has to be made: How much coverage should I (you) buy? Tally up all the debts you have, any lump sums of cash you want to provide (emergency fund for survivors, college funds for kids, etc.), and then add that total to the present value of the stream of income that would need to go to your heirs at your death. (Factor in their working ability, your confidence in Social Security, etc.). A competent financial advisor can work through this calculation with you. Usually, the resulting number suggests obtaining between seven and fifteen times your annual income, depending on all the variables.

TERM AND PERMANENT LIFE INSURANCE COVERAGE

> Essentially, there are two types of life insurance: term and permanent.

Essentially, there are two types of life insurance: term and permanent. *Term life insurance* is much like all other insurance coverage you might purchase. If you die, the insurance company pays a death claim. If the coverage lapses or is discontinued, there is no further value. *Permanent life insurance*, on the other hand, might build cash value. There are many types of permanent policies, and this is where the confusion often starts.

THE MORTALITY CURVE

The following graph is essentially a mortality curve. Term life insurance is priced based on such a mortality curve. You can buy a ten-, twenty-, or even thirty-year term policy whose rate is level for that time, but if you wanted to renew beyond that point, the rates would go up exponentially. Also, a *convertible* term policy (which allows you to convert from term to permanent without evidence of good health) is very appropriate for young physicians as a way to secure some coverage for a small premium while they are healthy and the rates are low and have the flexibility to change along the way, if they desire.

Types of Life Insurance and Product Pricing:

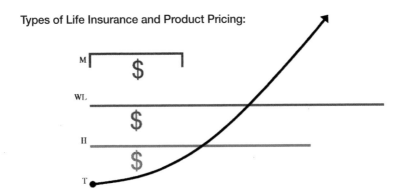

This is a very generic and simplified graph to illustrate the annual premium pricing differences among the main types of products. Individual circumstances and product design, coordinated by a knowledgeable and experienced advisor, will determine the final numbers. (M=MEC, WL=Whole Life, H=Hybrid, T=Term). Explained in surrounding paragraphs.

TERM LIFE INSURANCE

Term life insurance tends to be the most affordable way to cover a given risk. The length of term policies is typically anywhere between five and thirty years. Very simply, you get a policy that has a death benefit that fits your need for the length of time you desire. For example, a $1,000,000 ten-year term policy would provide a death benefit of $1,000,000 to your beneficiary if you pass away any time in years 1–10 of the policy. If you die in year 11, no death benefit would be passed on. Of course (as noted in the chart), if you stretch out the coverage period, the policy becomes more expensive. This means that a thirty-year term policy will be more expensive than a fifteen-year term policy.

There are additional features and riders you can add onto your policy to make it more robust; however, many of these will add cost to your policy. One feature we often recommend adding onto a term policy is a *conversion option* (which is free on many policies). This allows you to keep the coverage by converting it to a different type of policy at the end of your term period, if you choose. Whether or not you will want to convert the coverage at the end of your term, or any time in-between, depends on a number of factors, but we see a lot of value in having that option.

Ultimately, term insurance is the most inexpensive life insurance and the easiest to understand. Many physicians and physician families are properly covered with term insurance and choose not to purchase any permanent coverage at all. This is a very efficient route; it frees up cash flow for other opportunities and might be best for you. If you aren't sure where to begin with life insurance, or want to spend as little as possible, then it may be wise to speak with a professional about a convertible term policy with level premiums.

TWO TYPES OF PERMANENT LIFE INSURANCE: WHOLE AND HYBRID

As for permanent life insurance, there are many marketing names and varieties of policies. For practical purposes in this book, we will outline the two most common: whole life and a "hybrid" policy.

1. Whole Life

While products vary by provider, a simplified way to look at the whole life (Whole Life, WL) is that it was developed many years ago as an alternative to term insurance. The premium is much more expensive than term in the early years, but it becomes level throughout your life. Because you are paying more for the coverage than the pure risk while you are young, "cash value" is created for the purpose of helping to offset the increasing cost of coverage later in life. This is what helps support the cost for the life insurance when you are older, and the cost of insurance is actually more than the value of the premium you are paying. If you pay enough into the whole life policy, it can become paid up.

> Whole life insurance was developed as an alternative to term insurance.

Here are some advantages of whole life, besides the fact that it offers lifetime coverage:

1. The cash values grow on a tax-deferred basis.
2. You can surrender the policy if necessary.
3. You can use it as collateral if you need to borrow against it.

This multipurpose asset has gained in popularity in recent years because the cash values grow from one year to the next, based on a crediting rate paid by the insurance company.

> We have worked with people who have a dozen policies that duplicate policy fees, which is inefficient when you consider that other "hybrid" products exist.

The disadvantages of whole life are also numerous. For one thing, these policies are not very flexible. If you need to make changes to the policy (raising or lowering the death benefit or the premium amount), it can be cumbersome or impossible, depending on the company. Many companies would rather sell you a new policy rather than make changes to an existing policy, and that can potentially result in new or higher fees and commissions. We have run into people who have a dozen policies that duplicate policy fees, which is inefficient when you consider that other "hybrid" products exist. For people who are very conservative, have quite a bit of discretionary cash flow, are not comfortable investing in anything that has market risk, and have a need to ensure a death benefit for their entire life, a whole life policy might be appropriate.

2. "Hybrid" Policy

The "hybrid" (H) policy is another option in which the annual premium generally falls somewhere between term and whole life. This can vary quite a bit, and in general, the higher the premium, the more the opportunity for more cash value…resulting in the policy remaining in force for a longer period of time. The graph above illustrates a premium payment and coverage lasting until retirement age.

There are many different hybrid policies, which confuses the subject even more. Usually, the premium is flexible and changeable, the death benefit can vary as your needs change, and there are a variety of methods of crediting the cash-value accounts. In general, you can use this flexible choice to implement a part of a financial plan that you, the policy owner, monitors frequently, along with a trusted financial advisor.

Very conservative investors used to gravitate toward fixed life policies. An indexed product allows for a potential upside (with limitations) connected to a common benchmark (such as the S&P 500 index), while the downside is protected. A variable life policy allows the policy owner to build a portfolio often choosing between numerous sub accounts. You can be as conservative or aggressive as your own needs and circumstances allow. Of course, this carries market risk that is not present in traditional fixed or indexed insurance products. Because of

all of the options, working with an experienced advisor who knows you, your circumstances, and your risk tolerance is recommended.

When a policy is funded at a much higher level, it can build more cash value and, in some cases, become paid up. (In the diagram titled "Types of Life Insurance and Product Pricing" just presented, see the graph labeled "M.") There is an IRS calculation based on your age and death-benefit amount, and it determines the maximum premium you can pay without the policy becoming a Modified Endowment Contract (MEC), which then loses some valuable benefits.

Figuring out how much you want to contribute to a policy for all your personal reasons (tax-deferred growth, asset protection, funding for kids' college education, retirement supplement, etc.) and then determining the least amount of death benefit you need to have will result in a situation in which the policy works best for the long-term "living" reasons. Again, we cannot emphasize this enough: please work with a very competent agent or advisor on these matters because a mistake here could "taint" your policy, and you could lose some of the valuable tax benefits. Also, keep in mind that getting a minimal amount of permanent insurance while supplementing it with efficient term insurance might be the best way to go to get the most value out of each option.

Keep in mind that for many physician families, simply using term insurance is the most appropriate and efficient strategy. Consult with your financial professional to determine which option(s) are best for you.

Variable life insurance is sold only by prospectus. The prospectus contains important information about the product's investment objectives, charges and expenses, as well as the risks and other information associated with the product. You may obtain a copy of the prospectus from your representative. You should carefully consider the risks and investment charges of a specific product before investing. You should always read the prospectus carefully before investing.

Variable life insurance products contain fees, such as management fees, fund expenses, distribution fees, and mortality and expense charges. The variable investment options are subject to market risk, including loss of principal.

Policy loans and withdrawals may create an adverse tax result in the event of a lapse or policy surrender and will reduce both the cash value and death benefit.

If a policy is overfunded and becomes a modified endowment contract (MEC), the contract's earnings will be taxed as ordinary income at withdrawal and may be subject to a 10 percent penalty if withdrawn before age 59.5.

Please keep in mind that the primary reason to purchase a life insurance product is the death benefit.

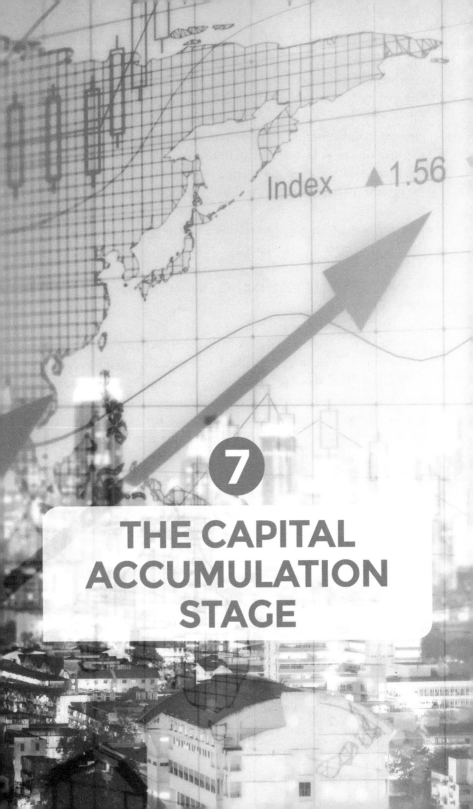

7

THE CAPITAL ACCUMULATION STAGE

Index ▲1.56

This stage represents a large amount of assets you will build up over your lifetime. The assets that tend to compose this stage are quite varied. Some of the investments include individual stocks and bonds, mutual funds, variable life insurance cash values, and equity in real estate or a business. Aside from the equity you build into your retirement plan, the majority of your financial independence will come from these investments. While these assets can also serve as emergency reserves, the investment horizon is usually five years or longer.

Let's explore the most important discussion points as you begin to develop your investment philosophy.

1. INVESTMENT PLANNING: INFORMATION VS. WISDOM

Over the years, we have seen many market cycles, wars, natural disasters, terrorist attacks, low interest rates, high interest rates, and innumerable other factors that have influenced our physician clients' investment performance. But what factors have had the biggest influence on long-term investment planning? What factors have led to success? What factors have contributed to failure? What are the prudent, time-tested investment strategies that will likely have the most positive influence on your overall long-term performance?

While there are numerous scenarios that will determine your investment success or failure, here is a brief summary of strategies we believe have the most potential to influence your long-term return on investment.

Diversify to Minimize Your Risk

As for setting up an investment portfolio...diversify, diversify, diversify! Nothing else will be as crucial to your portfolio as diversifying and having a long-term plan. It's important to diversity not only by asset class but also by tax treatment and time horizon. We all know the proverb, "Don't put all your eggs in one basket." Well, take it to the extreme—don't put all the baskets on the same truck, and don't drive all the trucks down the same road! We don't have to look too far back to recall the faddish investing in technology and startup internet companies of the late 1990s. Too many investors lost too much when the overvalued stocks plunged, and those eager investors expecting big returns were left with substantial losses. Most financial planners use a comprehensive questionnaire that helps you identify your risk tolerance, and ultimately your asset allocation policy. Be sure to ask your advisor for such a tool.

There are many factors that determine the performance of a particular investment from one year to the next. Individual asset-class performance can vary so much from year to year that trying to predict results will likely lead to poor decisions. A portfolio well diversified among many asset categories will have lower volatility and provide better potential for a steadier performance. Your overall returns might not be the highest or lowest in any given period, but by keeping volatility levels in check in the short term, you will reduce the likelihood of making irrational decisions that can have very harmful effects on your long-term returns.

> A portfolio well diversified among many asset categories will have lower volatility and provide better potential for a steadier performance.

Diversification is sometimes misunderstood. The main goal of diversification is not to *maximize* your return but to *minimize* your risk and *lower* your volatility. The basic premise is that there is as much risk in being out of the market when it goes up as there is being in the market when it goes down, especially for your long-term money. While diversification does not guarantee against loss, it is a method used to manage risk.

Focus on Time...Not Timing

You can help manage something very volatile, like the annual returns in the stock market, by adding the element of time. Although past performance is not a guarantee of future results, historically, the longer the time frame considered, generally, the less volatile an investment becomes. So one of the most important considerations for your financial plan is to keep your short-term (less than eighteen months) money away from the stock market and allocate your long-term (greater than ten years) money to a well-diversified portfolio of mostly equities.

Avoid Mainstream-Media Sensationalism

If you were to make investment decisions based on the nightly news, CNBC, or the daily newspaper, not only would you be destined for investment failure, but you might even face total destitution! This is *not* due to the inaccuracy of information being provided by such sources, but rather the dramatization of *short-term* events that have little or no impact on long-term investment strategies!

Using information that is reported daily for decisions with long-term money can have devastating consequences. This danger is compounded significantly by the ease with which you can simply log on to your brokerage account, 401(k) account, or any other investment account and make changes on a daily basis.

> Money invested for the long term should not be managed like it is needed next week. It must be managed with a long-term perspective.

Manage Behavior and Decisions

When discussing average rates of return over longer periods, it is important to differentiate between the average rate of return for the *investor* and that of the *fund*. The rate of return for the specific fund does not necessarily translate to the individual investor earning the same rate of return. An illustration can best emphasize this point on the futility of chasing rates of return.

One of our favorite market examples was reported by *The Wall Street Journal* on December 31, 2009.[8] The CGM Focus Fund was the best-performing equity fund throughout the decade that had just ended. Some describe it as the "lost decade" because the S&P 500 index had a compounded loss over the same time frame. The CGM Focus Fund had an average rate of return of 18 percent per year. Yet the average investor experienced an 11 percent *loss*! Why? Because they invested in the fund after a run-up in value, chased past returns, and sold when the fund was down, guaranteeing and locking in their losses. This is exactly the behavior that investors should avoid.

Avoid Concentrating on a Specific Asset Category

It's easy to pick on the scores of investors who were caught up in the tech boom of the late 1990s. Many who invested so heavily in technology became significantly overweighted in one asset category and then suffered devastating losses during the market down turn of 2000 to 2003.

---

8. "Best Stock Fund of the Decade: CGM Focus," December 31, 2009, *The Wall Street Journal*, https://www.gurufocus.com/news/80345/wsj-best-stock-fund-of-the-decade-cgm-focus. This example is being used for illustrative purposes only and is not a recommendation to invest in the CGM Focus Fund. Generally, potential for higher return is accompanied by a higher risk of loss. A fund's risks, expenses, investment objectives, and other information is available in the fund's prospectus. You should carefully consider the risks and investment charges of a specific product and carefully read the prospectus before investing.

It is so easy, in fact, that we won't. But what about investment periods of one, three, and five years, during which the performance variation among different asset categories is more subtle? What is the best method to manage a portfolio over time without getting too concentrated in one asset category or not having enough in another?

The first step is to diversify! There are many methods to help determine an appropriate allocation, given your specific time horizon, risk-tolerance level, and overall investment objectives. This process requires much discussion and thought, but ultimately, an allocation will emerge. You will discover what percentage of your investments should be allocated toward various asset categories, large cap growth, large cap value, international, fixed income, small cap, and so on.

> **The first step is to diversify!**

> It is critical to monitor this allocation regularly and determine when it is appropriate to alter new contributions or possibly even trim down one asset category to buy another.

There are two main objectives of regularly monitoring a diversified portfolio:

- **Keep target allocations in line with original allocations.** This will make it less likely to become over- or underweighted in one asset category. It also will decrease the likelihood of making investment decisions based on emotions.

- **Avoid overmonitoring.** The ease with which you can make changes to any investment makes it difficult to keep from reacting to short-term fluctuations. By regularly monitoring and discussing your portfolio, you can know where one particular fund is in the overall picture and determine a reasonable time or specific share price to reallocate.

Don't Expect Everything from One Investment

This is a long-winded equivalent to diversification. Building a prudent, well-structured investment portfolio consists of having exposure to assets with potential for big gains over time and to assets that perform consistently during good times while helping limit losses in bad times.

Having a mix of stocks and bonds is critical to lower levels of volatility over time. A well-allocated mix of investments consists of exposure to the following broad asset categories:

- Growth stocks: large, medium, and small[9]

- Value stocks: large, medium, and small

- International stocks[10]: developed countries, emerging markets

- Fixed income: corporate bonds, government bonds, high-yield bonds[11]

- Real estate securities[12]: low correlation with stocks

The percentage of exposure you have to each type of asset category will depend on your time horizon, risk profile, and overall objectives.

Once your allocation is established, regular monitoring and periodic rebalancing will be critical in helping you accomplish the two most important objectives: trying to achieve lower levels of short-term volatility and pursuing the highest potential for long-term rate of return.

---

9. Investments in smaller company and micro-cap stocks generally carry a higher level of volatility and risk over the short term.

10. Investment risks associated with international investing, in addition to other risks, include currency fluctuations, political and economic instability, and differences in accounting standards.

11. Fixed-income securities are subject to credit and interest rate risk and, as such, their value generally will fall as interest rates rise. High-yield, lower-rated (junk) bonds generally have greater price swings and higher default risks.

12. Investment risks associated with investing in the real estate fund/portfolio, in addition to other risks, include rental-income fluctuation, depreciation, property-tax value changes, and differences in real estate market values.

Get Help from a Professional

While we like to think and tell our clients how good we are at "picking" the right investments, this is not how an investment professional adds real, meaningful value. Yes, a true professional is generally better equipped to analyze investment vehicles more thoroughly than the average physician, but this is not what will have the biggest influence on your investment rate of return. An advisor can provide great value to your investment strategy through a fee-based Investment Advisory account.

So, where and how does an advisor add real value?

> An advisor can provide great value to your investment strategy through a fee-based Investment Advisory account. He or she also can add significant value to your investment planning by helping you deal with emotional decisions.

A financial advisor worth his or her weight in gold is one who is not afraid to tell you "No" when it comes to making investment decisions based on emotion. It is your hard-earned money and your future, and you are emotionally attached to it. When the value investment goes up in one quarter or even a year, you cannot help but want to buy more of it. What better "source" for this than selling an investment *down* in value during

the same time period? Tempting as it is, this strategy of decision making based predominantly on a short-term trend and/or a "gut feeling" will almost certainly lead to disappointing long-term returns.

Your advisor should take the time to discuss the specifics of why each fund is performing the way it is during this short time period, what it means to the overall objective of your portfolio, and whether you need to make any decisions to buy or sell some or all of the fund.

Many times, in our experience, just talking a bit further about a particular fund's performance and gaining a better understanding of the reasons behind the performance will be enough to avoid emotional and many times irrational decisions that can have a devastating effect on your portfolio's long-term performance.

Your advisor should regularly update you on your portfolio's progress, review your *current* asset allocation with that of your *target* allocation, and discuss potential adjustments you should make. Adjustments to your investment portfolio are based on many factors, not just on recent performance. Changes in your income or overall debt, upcoming purchases, job changes, and family life changes can be relevant to your investment portfolio.

> Adjustments to your investment portfolio are based on many factors, not just on recent performance.

Simply put, it is important to be "in tune" with changes in your life and how they relate to your investment portfolio and necessary adjustments to it.

Doing so will help ensure that such alterations are based on sound fundamentals, not on short-term events that will have little impact on your long-term objectives.

Factor in Investment Fees

Expenses play an influential role in underlying performance, but sometimes discussions and opinions about them miss the mark.

Expenses come in many forms: 12b-1 fees, management fees, expense ratios, trade or transaction costs, and so on. You can pick up almost any investment-related trade journal or magazine and see that expenses are on investors' minds and play a big role in their decisions. It goes without saying that if Fund X has a lower total expense than Fund Y, and performance over a given time period for each fund is the same, investors in Fund X will have a higher *net* return. From this perspective, expenses will always play a significant role in an investment's rate of return.

However, these types of discussions go beyond the old adage "Cheaper is better," just as information and easy access to it does not always translate into wise decision making. In other words, if Fund Y is more expensive than Fund X, what are the expenses for it, and how do the factors that *make* it more expensive influence return?

Nowadays you can build a very well-diversified portfolio using low-cost, passive index funds, for example. In general, it's wise to be fee-conscious when looking at your portfolio. We prefer low cost as frequently as we can; however, there are occasional scenarios in which being a little more tactical with investments or specialty market sectors can also make sense.

In general, there is nothing inherently wrong with paying a management fee to an investment advisor. This is true especially if you aren't comfortable managing capital gains, rebalancing, executing tax loss harvesting, doing due diligence, etc. Maybe you simply don't have the time, discipline, or capacity to give your investment portfolio the attention it deserves. What is more important is that you know these two things:

- How much you are paying in fees
- The valuable service you are receiving for the amount you are paying

In summary, it is important to understand the fees inside your portfolio. Minimize fees where you can. Your investment advisor should be able to clearly identify and explain these fees for you, and you should feel comfortable with his or her explanation. Finally, remember what you are trying to accomplish: a properly diversified portfolio with the best net return.

Include Dividends in Your Portfolio

The Jobs and Growth Tax Relief Reconciliation Act of 2003 provided a nice benefit for higher-income medical specialists. In years past, investing in companies that pay dividends to shareholders has been somewhat of a tax problem for physicians in a high tax bracket. Dividends were taxed as ordinary income, which, for the high-income specialist, translated to a lower rate of return than for someone in a lower tax bracket receiving dividend income.

> Dividend income can be a very important component of your total return, so it is essential to own such stocks within your overall portfolio.

The Jobs and Growth Tax Relief Reconciliation Act *lowered* the tax rate for qualified dividends to 15 percent. This tax treatment remains in

effect for most people in 2018. However, for high-income specialists (those in the top tax bracket), the rate is 20 percent plus a 3.8 percent tax, for a total of 23.8 percent. In either case, this means that instead of keeping less than two-thirds of any dividend income, you will now retain somewhere be-tween 80 and 85 percent!

> In your planning, it is important to remember that tax laws are subject to change.

Use Bonds and Fixed-Income Investments to Lower Volatility

It is easy to compare the annual average rate of return of stocks with that of bonds and assume that stocks, with their higher long-term average return, is where the vast majority of your long-term investments should be. *Diversification* among asset categories means having exposure to investments that are not correlated. Bond and fixed-income investments are influenced by different factors than stocks and will perform differently in different market cycles. Having exposure to bonds will again lower your portfolio's volatility levels in the short term and make it less likely to commit impulsive short-term investment decisions with your long-term investments.

Invest Monthly for Dollar Cost Averaging

An additional strategy to employ when investing is *dollar cost averaging*, which is the process of investing a fixed amount of money each month (or quarter, or year) without worrying about whether the market is up or down. When it is down, you will buy more shares, bringing your average share price down. Over time, besides the element of forced savings, the tendency to try to outguess the market and purchase shares at the ideal moment is eliminated. Dollar cost averaging does not assure a profit, nor does it protect against loss in declining markets. This investment strategy requires regular investments, regardless of the fluctuating price of the investment. Consider your financial ability to continue investing during periods of low price levels.

> Dollar cost averaging requires regular investments.

Rebalance Your Asset Mix Regularly

When you have a large amount of money to invest, coming up with an investment policy and adhering to it is a must. Once you choose an overall asset allocation mix based on your goals and objectives, stick to it. Change it only if there are significant changes in the economy, the portfolio, and/or your goals and objectives.

> Then, on a regular basis (either quarterly, semiannually, or annually), *rebalance* the portfolio back to the asset allocation you started with.

With this strategy, your investment mix does not get skewed toward more or less risk or volatility. Many portfolio managers have the capability of providing this rebalancing process on an automatic basis.

A well-balanced portfolio is properly diversified by the following asset decisions:

- Stocks vs. bonds
- United States (domestic) investment vs. international securities
- Large cap versus small cap stocks
- Growth vs. value stocks (Keep this in balance!)
- Short-, medium-, and long-term investments

There are many good resources that will help you take this process much further than the scope of this book. We think some of the best information can come from a competent and qualified financial advisor who will listen to you and develop a plan that meets your needs.

In general, a higher investment risk is best for those who:

- Can accept short-term losses
- Believe gains will offset losses over the long run
- Will not leave the investment if one or two bad years occur
- Have a long "investment time horizon"

Learn from the Experts

The best way to learn sound market advice is to listen to the experts. The following quotes from mutual fund leaders all stress the futility of market timing:

Peter Lynch: "My single-most important piece of investment advice is to ignore the short-term fluctuations of the market. From one year to the next, the stock market is a coin flip. It can go up or down. The real money in stocks is made in the third, fourth, and fifth year of your investments because you are participating in a company's earnings, which grow over time."

Warren Buffet: "I do not have, never have had, and never will have an opinion where the stock market will be a year from now."

Sir John Templeton: "Ignore fluctuations. Do not try to outguess the stock market. Buy a quality portfolio, and invest for the long term."

So, to drive it home, invest for the long term, and be patient!

2. PHYSICIAN MORTGAGE AND HOME BUYING

For many Americans, one of the most substantial forms of saving is simply making a monthly payment on their homes. Generally speaking, real estate has long been a favorite investment tool for its tax benefits and as a buffer against inflation. Although there can be significant investment benefits in the long term, buying real estate is not without risks. Deflation and poor housing markets can decrease property values, or suspected long-term growth in a given area might not occur. Changes in tax laws can reduce or eliminate anticipated tax benefits. Also, real estate is not liquid, so the necessity of a quick sale can require you to reduce the price substantially.

Buying a home is quite possibly one of the biggest financial decisions you can make. Your home might be the place you raise your kids, spend the majority of your time, and create lasting memories. It might also be the linchpin to the rest of your financial budget. The choices made when you purchase a home will likely dictate how much you can save for retirement, your kids' education, vacations, etc. For this reason, creating an appropriate plan that takes into consideration how your mortgage fits into your budget is essential.

Work with a mortgage professional to determine the right financing option for you. This step should not be overlooked. In this chapter, we take you through the most common financing opportunities available to physicians. Keep in mind that each individual situation is different, and each housing market/location can be dramatically different. The best strategy for you might differ from the approaches listed below. We strongly encourage you to work with a trusted financial professional who can help you determine an appropriate home budget and review your specific financing opportunities.

Budgeting

Determining how much home you can afford can vary dramatically from city to city and from market to market. Put plenty of thought into other required obligations you have, like student loan payments, for example.

> In general, however, if you live in a reasonable market (excluding DC, San Francisco, New York, and similar markets), we like to think a good target to shoot for with regard to a home purchase budget is two to two and a half times your gross income.

So if you are a hospitalist making $200,000 per year with a spouse who does not work, we recommend shooting for a home priced under $500,000, and preferably closer to the $400,000 mark or less, if possible. It's important to keep this number in mind because if you shop for mortgages with a banker or mortgage broker, it's likely that they will "approve" you for well over this amount. Keep in mind that these people get paid on your purchase size—the larger mortgage you take, the more they get paid. For this reason, a banker's version of what you can truly afford is likely much higher than what a financial professional feels you can afford. A prudent planner also knows you need to pay down student loans, save for retirement, and pursue other financial goals.

> A banker's version of what you can truly afford is likely much higher than what a financial professional feels you can afford.

When calculating what your mortgage payment will be based on home size, you will also want to consider a number of additional factors. Your home could come with a required homeowners' association (HOA) fee. You will have property taxes to consider, and homeowner's insurance should be factored in as well. Fortunately, there are a number of free calculators online that you can use to estimate the actual cost of a mortgage and these additional expenses.

Types of Mortgages

There are a number of types of mortgages to consider, so be sure to speak with a mortgage professional regarding all the options available to you. You can get a fixed rate or an adjustable rate, you can choose the duration of the loan (fifteen or thirty years, for example), and you can decide to use traditional lending or physician-specific options. Also, you will need to decide how much your down payment will be, which is usually anywhere between zero and 20 percent of the home's value. In this chapter, we explain these decisions and the strategy behind making the right choice.

- **Fixed or variable/adjustable rates**—Adjustable-rate mortgages tend to show lower interest rates on your mortgage for a determined amount of time, but they can increase after that period expires. For example, you might find a 5/1 adjustable rate mortgage (ARM) advertised somewhere. This means that for the first five years of the mortgage, the interest rate is fixed. After that, the rate can increase, depending on the current interest-rate environment and market conditions.

  As of the writing of this book, we are in a very low-interest-rate environment. While nobody knows what the future holds, most experts agree that interest rates will increase over the coming years. For that reason, we are fans of locking in a *fixed interest rate* for the long haul. That way, if interest rates do rise over time, you won't need to worry about the rate on your mortgage increasing simultaneously.

  > We are fans of locking in a *fixed interest rate* for the long haul.

  The exception to this rule would be for a shorter duration. For example, you can lock in a 7/1 ARM with a lower interest rate than a thirty-year fixed mortgage if you plan to stay in your house for only five years (during residency and/or fellowship, for example). In this situation, the ARM might make sense because you will be selling prior to the potential rate increase in year 8.

- **The case for choosing a thirty-year fixed instead of a fifteen-year fixed rate.** Now that we have determined that a fixed-rate mortgage is likely the route to go, the next choice is to decide on the duration of that rate. Should you go with a thirty-year mortgage or a fifteen-year mortgage? If your goal is to pay as little in interest as possible, then the fifteen-year option makes sense. However, if your goal is to create as much wealth as possible over time, a good case can be made for a thirty-year fixed rate. Here are a few reasons behind that choice:

- **Your mortgage interest is deductible**[13]—As a physician, you are likely in the top 5 percent of income earners in the country, which means that taxes are a big deal for you. Mortgage interest paid per year is tax-deductible, which means the quicker you pay off your mortgage, the quicker you are getting rid of one of the best tax-deduction tools you have!

- **You're allocating money toward a low-interest debt.** Consider paying down your mortgage this way. When you allocate money toward a debt (like a mortgage), you are getting a return on your investment of the interest rate on that debt. As we discussed, we are in a very low-interest-rate environment. So, let's say your mortgage interest is 4 percent. Subtract the tax deductibility; now it's maybe a 3 percent debt. Paying more toward your mortgage is essentially getting you a 3 percent rate of return on your money. Wouldn't your money be better suited going toward your student loans at a much higher rate? Or even being allocated toward retirement or long-term investment growth?

- **Traditional lending or physician mortgages**—For "regular" people to qualify for a home mortgage, they typically need to put down a pretty healthy down payment. In fact, if they don't put down at least 20 percent, they will need to pay PMI (private mortgage insurance), which is essentially

---

13. In 2018, mortgage interest deductions were capped at $750,000. Consult with a tax professional to confirm the potential benefits of mortgage interest deduction.

paying for the bank's insurance. This fee can vary based on a number of factors, but it is often somewhere between 0.5 and 1.5 percent of the original loan amount per year.

> Fortunately, there are "physician" or "doctor" mortgage programs that allow you to put as little as zero percent down and still avoid paying PMI.

Why is this possible? Simply put, banks want your business. In general, the default rate on physician mortgages is lower than the overall default rate, which is why banks are willing to offer this benefit. Essentially, you are getting rewarded for your peers paying their bills.

o **How much should you put down?**—The answer to this question is complicated. However, if you're a young physician just finishing up residency or fellowship (or in training now), you likely don't have 10 to 20 percent available to immediately allocate toward a down payment. For doctors in this camp, less is more, and taking advantage of one of the low-to-zero percent-down options is likely a good play. Keep in mind, you can always put more into the house later if you want.

For everyone else, keep in mind what was previously discussed. Every dollar you're allocating toward your low interest mortgage is a dollar that could be going to something that has a higher potential return.

> For this reason, if interest rates are still incredibly low for mortgages, keeping your down payment low can be the most efficient financial move.

- **Other factors to consider**—As mentioned, there are a number of variables to consider, and the information in this chapter is a generalized overview. In addition to the items listed above, here are some other factors worth considering.

  - **Plan to own for at least five years**—A general rule of thumb for buying a home is that you should plan to own the home for a minimum of five years. The reason for this is in the math. When you look at an amortization schedule (how your payments are allocated), you will notice that the vast majority of your mortgage payments, on the front end, go toward interest, not principal. So if you plan on selling in less than five years, most of your money has gone toward interest, not toward increasing your equity in the home. Also, there are also fees and commissions that you will incur when buying and selling. Closing costs, Realtor fees, etc., can eat into what you thought was going to be profit on the sale.

  - **Your credit score is important**—Your credit score will play a big role in the interest rate you get on your mortgage. Do what you can to optimize your score before you shop for mortgages.

    POOR   GOOD

  - **Origination fees can be negotiated**—There isn't a ton that you can negotiate with mortgage contracts, but origination fees are often negotiable. Often, you can get this fee removed, which can save thousands of dollars on your overall purchase.

  - **There are state-by-state options**—Every state has different options when it comes to mortgages. So if you used a bank for your first mortgage in residency and have since moved to a different location, it's likely you will need to use a completely new bank (although many can offer lending in multiple states).

Financial advisors do not provide specific mortgage advice and do not extend home loans. Be sure to work with a mortgage professional regarding your personal situation. This section is for educational purposes only, as it applies to personal finance and budgeting. It should not be considered mortgage advice.

8

THE TAX-ADVANTAGED STAGE

Because you are a physician, the government likes you! Therefore, the main objective of the tax-advantaged stage is to try to significantly delay, reduce, and/or minimize the impact of taxes on your financial picture. Why? To accumulate and create the highest net worth you possibly can.

DELAY TAX BY PUTTING MONEY IN A QUALIFIED RETIREMENT PLAN

One method of delaying tax involves investing dollars in qualified retirement plans. This means the dollars are contributed on a before-tax (qualified) basis. Again, the taxes are not eliminated; they are just deferred until you withdraw the funds. These plans include individual retirement accounts (IRAs), simplified employee pensions (SEPs), tax-sheltered annuities (TSAs), pension and profit-sharing plans, and 401(k)/403(b) plans.

> The main objective of this stage is to try to significantly delay, reduce, and/or minimize the impact of taxes on your financial picture.

The main advantage behind these plans is that the government has given you a significant motivation to save money because your taxable income is reduced dollar for dollar by the contribution. That, in turn, reduces your current tax liability, subject to limitations, depending on your income. In other words, your adjusted gross income will be less, which means your taxable income is reduced for the tax year.

Although these accounts are good places to defer and delay tax liability during your working years, they present some problems at retirement because the taxes become due then. Also, transferring qualified assets to heirs can present some tax nightmares if not handled carefully.

> The general principle here is to save money in these plans when you are in a higher tax bracket and withdraw the funds at retirement, when you are in a lower tax bracket.

Early in your career, or when you are still completing your residency or fellowship, and your income and tax bracket are low, it doesn't make any sense to put a lot of money into an IRA or 401(k) plan. Why defer money when you are in the lowest tax bracket you will ever be in? You might want to contribute to a 401(k) just up to where the employer matches those funds, and then take advantage of a Roth IRA for as long as your income allows you to contribute.

CONSIDER A TAX-ADVANTAGED ROTH IRA

As of 2018, a Roth IRA allows you to contribute up to $5,500 per year on an after-tax basis. These accounts do not provide any tax relief today. The advantage of a Roth IRA is that all investment earnings grow tax-deferred, and provided that certain requirements are met, all distributions after age 59½ are withdrawn *tax-free*. (There is a 10 percent IRS penalty for distributions taken within the first five years or prior to age 59½.)

So you can forgo the tax break when in a lower tax bracket and withdraw gains tax-free at a time when you may be in a much higher tax environment. There is value in contributing to a Roth IRA throughout your career; however, it takes some creativity. More on this later in the chapter.

An investor's anticipated tax bracket in retirement will determine whether or not a Roth IRA versus a traditional IRA will provide more money in retirement. Generally, investors who are in a higher tax bracket at retirement relative to their current tax bracket while making contributions to a Roth IRA benefit more than an investor who is in a lower tax bracket at retirement.

Our intention here is not to give an in-depth description of every type of qualified plan available, but rather to provide a brief description of each option to help you understand basic terms and definitions associated with each plan. Here are some highlights of qualified plans:

- Tax-deductible contributions
- Tax-deferred growth of investment earnings
- Most protected from claims of creditors (Make sure you speak with your attorney.)

Here are some drawbacks of qualified plans:

- Plan assets are generally illiquid until you reach age 59½. (A 10 percent IRS penalty applies to distributions prior to age 59½.)
- Annual contributions can be restrictive, in particular for the high-income medical specialist.
- All distributions are taxed as ordinary income.
- Complexity of plan design, set-up, and administration fees can be high.

Here is a brief discussion of the various employer retirement plans.

1. EMPLOYER RETIREMENT PLANS

SIMPLE IRAs

A SIMPLE IRA is generally a good option for a practice with a small number of employees. ("SIMPLE" is an acronym that stands for "savings incentive match for employees.") A SIMPLE IRA allows all employees to contribute a portion of their salary each paycheck and also requires that an employer contribution be made on behalf of all eligible employees.

Current guidelines allow each employee to set aside up to $12,500 ($15,500 if age fifty or over) in 2018. Contributions made to the plan are 100 percent tax-deductible. In addition, the employer or practice owner must *either* match employee contributions dollar for dollar up to 3 percent of an employee's compensation *or* make a contribution of 2 percent of compensation for all eligible employees, regardless of whether they are contributing their own money to the plan.

SIMPLE IRAs are easy to set up, very inexpensive to administer, and very attractive for owners of smaller medical practices looking to offer a qualified retirement plan without a lot of cost or hassle.

401(k) Plans and 403(b) Plans

These plans are similar. The basic difference is that a 401(k) plan is used by for-profit companies, while a 403(b) is used by nonprofit companies, religious groups, school districts, and governmental organizations. The law allows these organizations to be exempt from certain administrative processes that apply to 401(k) plans. This means that administrative costs for a 403(b) are lower.

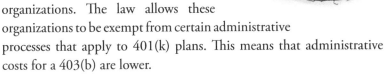

With a 401(k) or 403(b) plan, employees of your practice may choose to defer up to $18,500 ($24,500 if age fifty or over) annually into the plan on a pre-tax basis as of 2018. In addition, as the employer, you may elect to contribute a portion into the individual employee's account. If you have a 401(k) with a 3 percent match, assuming an income of $160,000, the total funding could be $23,300 ($18,500 + [$160,000 x 3 percent] = $23,300). Your practice may place a vesting schedule on the matching contributions. The physician/employee would be required to remain with the group a certain number of years for the matching contribution to "vest." Here is a summary of 401(k) plan benefits:

- High contribution limits for the employer and employees
- A competitive plan to attract and retain key people
- Loan provisions for hardships and emergencies
- Flexibility with respect to matching contributions

Both 401(k) and 403(b) plans have some similar characteristics to a SIMPLE IRA, but they have higher administrative costs and can vary significantly in their complexity. A very common problem with 401(k) and 403(b) plans is varying levels of employee deferral rates. If the higher-paid physicians contribute a significantly higher percentage of their income compared to lower-paid employees, the plan can be considered "top-heavy." This means too much money is in the accounts of the higher-paid physicians and will restrict the amount of money the physicians can defer into the plan. This problem can be addressed by adopting a safe harbor 401(k) plan.

Safe Harbor 401(k) Plans

A *safe harbor 401(k) plan* is intended to encourage plan participation among all employees and ease the administrative burden by eliminating IRS tests normally required with a traditional 401(k) plan.

A safe harbor 401(k) plan allows employees to contribute a percentage of their pay into the plan. It then requires an employer contribution of 3 percent of compensation on behalf of all eligible employees, whether they are participating in the plan or not. This contribution is also always immediately vested.

Another way to qualify as a safe harbor 401(k) is to match 100 percent of participant contributions up to 3 percent of pay, plus an additional 50 percent of participant contributions up to the next 2 percent of pay.

Such plans are ideal for a medical practice with highly compensated specialists whose contribution levels would be restricted with the traditional 401(k) plan. A safe harbor 401(k) can be a good fit for a medical practice that:

- Expects low participation by non-highly compensated employees
- Desires the highest limits for employee contributions
- Has very predictable and consistent cash flow to make the mandatory contribution each year
- Wants to eliminate the cost and burden of IRS testing
- Wants lower administrative expenses than with traditional 401(k)s

Roth 401(k)

A Roth 401(k) is a somewhat new type of retirement plan that combines the tax treatment of a Roth IRA with the annual contribution limits of a traditional 401(k). If you are a medical specialist, you might opt to take advantage of the Roth 401(k) if you are currently in a lower tax environment today than you likely will be in retirement. Such a plan allows you to contribute up to $18,500 annually on an after-tax basis, as of 2018. In other words, there is no tax benefit today associated with the contributions. However, the plan assets grow 100 percent tax-deferred and, provided certain requirements are met, you can withdraw all plan assets on a tax-free basis after age 59½.

> A younger medical specialist might be wise to opt for the Roth 401(k) for the first years after entering private practice when income and tax brackets are likely lower, and switch to the traditional 401(k) plan when income and associated tax levels increase significantly.

Profit-Sharing Plans

Profit-sharing plans are designed to allow employers to contribute to the plan on a discretionary basis. Depending on the terms of the plan, there is no set amount an employer needs to contribute each year. If contributions are made, you must have a set formula for determining how they are allocated among all eligible plan participants.

The maximum combined contribution limit the employer can deduct is 25 percent of total eligible payroll. (The maximum income per employee for consideration in 2018 is $275,000.) The maximum amount that you can allocate to an employee's account is 100 percent of total annual pay, or $55,000 in 2018, whichever is less. No employee deferrals are allowed without adding a 401(k) feature.

With a profit-sharing plan, the main benefit to the practice owner is the flexible nature of the contributions. It is possible to adjust contributions each year, depending on profitability of the clinic, as long as contributions are frequent and ongoing. A real, tangible benefit of a profit-sharing plan for the employee is having contributions to the plan tied to the performance and overall profitability of the clinic.

Money Purchase Plans

A *money purchase plan* is very similar to a profit-sharing plan in terms of contribution limits, benefits to the employer and employees, set-up and ongoing administrative costs, and eligibility. The primary difference is that employer contribution is a plan requirement. This amount is stated in the plan document.

> The benefit of a money purchase plan for you as the employer is that your fixed annual contributions to the plan make it easier to budget for and offer a measure of comfort and predictability for your employees.

But the inflexibility is often a big enough drawback that most practices gravitate to the other choices. It is beyond the scope of this text, but for certain situations (i.e., having a small number of employees with one or two older and highly paid specialists), a money purchase plan and/or a variation of it can provide for sizable annual deferral limits that exceed the other plans. Consult with a financial planner and tax advisor who specialize in working with high-income physicians to work with you on this decision.

Simplified Employee Pension (SEP) IRAs

A SEP IRA is a retirement plan that looks much like a profit-sharing plan. The contribution limit is 25 percent of employee compensation, up to a maximum of $55,000 in 2018. The administrative costs associated with a SEP IRA are very minimal, as are reporting and tax-filing requirements. The plan must cover all employees who have worked for the group in three of the past five years and are twenty-one years of age or older. SEP IRA plans are attractive for medical groups that have unpredictable cash flow because contributions to the plan can vary or not be made at all, depending on profitability. The contributions are 100 percent employer-paid, with no employee contributions allowed.

> SEP IRAs can also be particularly attractive for the medical specialist who has self-employment income from moonlighting or by working as an independent contractor.

Contributions for self-employment income are based on net income minus 50 percent of self-employment taxes paid and any deductible plan contributions, or a maximum of $55,000 in 2018. Because self-employment income is taxed very heavily, such a plan can be a very effective tool to lessen your tax burden. In addition, SEP plans can provide creditor protection at both the federal and state levels. Discuss this with your attorney.

In summary, qualified plans are an integral part of your retirement, and there are many ways you can design a plan. When your income is at the highest tax bracket, we generally advocate taking full advantage of the plan available to you through your employer and contributing the maximum annual contribution limit

> Qualified plans are an integral part of your retirement.

allowable under current tax law. If you are either joining a newer practice or starting your own practice and have questions or concerns regarding the existing plan or a new plan, we encourage you to contact a competent financial advisor for several reasons:

- Your qualified plan will likely be your largest retirement asset, so it should be carefully invested and monitored.

- Tax laws surrounding such plans have changed considerably and continue to change each year. This requires more time on your part to ensure that you have the most appropriate plan that provides you maximum benefit, given your circumstances.

- Tax arbitrage planning opportunities exist. You should invest in a qualified plan at a high tax bracket and withdraw the funds at a lower bracket. Your retirement income will likely come from several sources as you design a retirement income strategy to maximize your after-tax income.

2. INDIVIDUAL SAVINGS/RETIREMENT PLANS

Roth IRA Strategies to Consider

As previously discussed, Roth IRAs make a ton of sense while you're in a low tax bracket—say, in residency, fellowship, or very early in your career. A Roth allows you to pay taxes in your current tax bracket and then take both your contribution and any growth out tax-free at retirement.

> We encourage you to max out your qualified plan from your employer.

But what about while you're in your peak earning years? Can a Roth IRA still make sense? Our opinion is yes; however, some considerations need to be made before funding this correctly. First, as noted, we encourage you to max out your qualified plan from your employer. This can vary a bit, but let's just say that's $18,500 per year. There is a good chance you can do that and still want to save money elsewhere, intended for retirement. A Roth IRA makes sense, then, right? Well, the short answer is yes. However, you likely aren't eligible, at least without being a little, let's say, creative.

The IRS set an income threshold for eligibility to "directly" contribute to a Roth IRA. This number varies depending on your tax-filing status, but if you're in-practice, you are likely making too much. In 2018, the phase-out starts at $120,000 of modified adjusted gross income for single filers and at $189,000 for those who are married filing jointly.

You make too much money, so why are we still writing about this? Well, the answer is the *creative* part of planning referenced earlier. You'll notice that we intentionally italicized the word "directly" in the previous paragraph.

The IRS does limit your ability, as a high-income earner, to directly contribute to a Roth IRA. What they did not do was limit your ability to "convert" money into a Roth IRA.

This opens the door for a creative planner to get you access to a Roth IRA. This strategy is often referenced as a "back-door Roth IRA" or "Roth conversion strategy," and quite honestly, the execution is pretty simple. Here's how it works.

First you open a nondeductible/traditional IRA, ensuring that you do not take any deductions on your contribution. Once the assets are securely in that account, you can convert these dollars into a Roth IRA. You did not "directly" contribute to a Roth IRA at all; instead, you "converted" money into a Roth IRA. The maximum contribution remains the same ($5,500 per year in 2018). Here are some other scenarios to be aware of:

1. If you have a traditional IRA, this strategy might not work because there are a lot of taxation issues to be aware of. This really works only if you use an empty traditional IRA as the holding vehicle.

2. There should not be growth in the traditional IRA when you add the funds; therefore, consider keeping your contribution in "cash."

3. You will want to file Form 8606 with your taxes (to report nondeductible contributions you made to traditional IRAs). Discuss this with your accountant or tax professional.

Please note that this is a simplified abbreviation of this strategy. Careful consideration should be made before executing a back-door Roth IRA, and you should consult with a financial and/or tax professional.

Use Health Savings Accounts to Your Advantage

The final tax-advantaged strategy we will discuss in this chapter is a unique and incredibly underused opportunity surrounding health savings accounts (HSAs). The initial intent of the HSA was to offer a tax-favored way of saving for qualified medical expenses for those using a high-deductible health plan (HDHP). Over time, the use and strategy surrounding these accounts have evolved into what is now one of the most advantageous savings vehicles you have access to.

To qualify for an HSA, you must have a HDHP, which is defined as a health plan that has a minimum annual deductible of $1,350 for individuals and $2,700 for families (2018 figures). You also must be considered pre-Medicare benefits (not eligible), and you cannot be eligible to be claimed on someone else's tax return.

> If you enroll in Medicare Part A and/or B, you cannot contribute to your HSA. However, you may continue to withdraw money from your HSA after you enroll in Medicare to help pay for medical expenses, such as deductibles, premiums, copayments, and coinsurances. If you use the account for qualified medical expenses, its funds will continue to be tax-free.

If you're eligible for an HSA, you can start saving money into this account, and when done properly, get a triple tax-advantaged benefit. Here's why:

1. Contributions are exempt from federal taxation.

2. Interest/earnings will grow tax-deferred (you won't owe taxes on the growth).

3. Withdrawals for eligible expenses are exempt from federal taxation (more on this coming up).

Money that goes into an HSA plan can be invested like a 401(k) or IRA (assuming you have good investment options with your plan). Unlike flexible saving accounts (FSAs), those dollars can be carried over year after year, and they are yours to keep, even if you leave your employer.

So, up to this point, you can save the money tax-exempt and have it grow tax-deferred, but eventually you will want/need to use the money in your HSA.

While medical expenses allow you to pull the money out without taxation, another option to consider is to continue funding the account and letting it grow for as long as possible. At age sixty-five, you will be eligible for Medicare. You can use your HSA dollars to pay your Medicare expenses and premiums tax-free (but you can't pay insurance premiums prior to age sixty-five with HSA dollars).

Given the unique tax savings and future flexibility, it is likely a very wise play to start maxing out an HSA if you have access to one. Although this might be the most beneficial investment vehicle (from a tax-savings standpoint) that exists, many people aren't maxing it out, and many aren't using it at all.

3. CALCULATING YOUR TAX BRACKET

Just for you, we have taken the ten-thousand-page tax code and narrowed it down to one page. (See the "Basic Federal Tax Estimator"

later in this chapter.) Wouldn't it be nice if preparing our taxes were this easy! This is, of course, a basic guide only, just for education purposes, It doesn't factor in some of the specifics such as child care, student loan interest deductions, moving expenses, and so on. But, surprisingly, this is fairly accurate in estimating your federal tax liability.

We encourage you to work with your accountant or to run one of the tax software packages any time you have a major change in your life that will affect your taxes. As a helpful approximation, the guide here should provide a good planning estimate. Family changes such as a birth, death, or marriage all affect the tax you owe. Financial changes such as starting a new job, getting a raise, going back to school, and buying or moving to a new house will also impact your tax liability, and a new calculation should be made.

> **Compare your calculation to the amount you are having withheld from your paycheck. If you are withholding too much, change this amount with your employer by filling out a new W-4 form.**

This is especially useful for most everyone whose incomes adjust in accordance with their training. In July or August, you might start your employment and/or have a scheduled increase in your income or become a partner. If you don't work with your employer on the correct tax withholding, they will take out an amount that would correspond to your working for the whole year. Generally, there are many expenses, and having a higher take-home pay would most likely be more beneficial than getting a tax refund the following spring.

Getting a large refund isn't really that smart.

There are some important basic points to understand about taxes. First, getting a large refund isn't really that smart. It means you just gave the government an interest-free loan for the year. If you are a terrible saver and use this as a forced savings plan, we're guessing it still backfires on you because you know the lump-sum tax refund is coming, and you have plans for spending that amount, too! In any event, we suggest that you estimate your tax liability in advance and try to end up about even. That avoids any under-withholding penalties and any unexpected tax liability due that you might not be prepared for.

The second point is that it is always in your best interest to make more money! We've heard people say, "I just got a raise, and it jumped me into the next tax bracket, so I'm going to take home less!" That's not how it works. The tax system is a progressive tax, and the more income you make, the more you take home. It's just that each additional dollar is taxed at a higher percentage, but the first dollars are taxed the same. So moving into a higher tax bracket affects the last of your dollars you earn, but the first dollars are still taxed at the same rate.

For example, let's look at the Basic Federal Tax Estimator on the next few pages. Plug in your income (wages, interest income, etc.), and subtract contributions to pretax accounts to get your adjusted gross income. From that amount, subtract your personal exemptions and either the standard deduction or your itemized deductions, whichever is higher. Then look up your tax bracket on the chart.

The tax bracket is the tax on each additional dollar you earn, or the tax that is saved by virtue of reducing your taxable income by $1.

Suppose you are married, filing jointly, and your taxable income is $315,000. Your neighbors' taxable income comes in at $315,001 − $1 more, bumping them into the 32 percent tax bracket. Bummer for them, right? Yes and no. Their tax liability is only 32 cents more than yours because each new dollar is taxed at the 32 percent rate. They still have a take-home pay of 68 cents more than you, so while they are at a higher tax bracket, their take-home pay is more.

Your total tax is calculated as follows:

	The tax is:
First $19,050 of taxable income:	$1,905 (19,050 × .1)
$19,050 to $77,400 of taxable income:	$7,002 (58,350 × .12)
$77,400 to $165,000 of taxable income:	$19,272 (87,600 × .22)
$165,000 to $315,000 of taxable income:	$36,000 (150,000 × .24)
Total Federal Tax:	**$64,179**

Your neighbors' tax bill would be calculated the same as yours, with another 32 cents of tax liability on the $1 above $315,000 at the 32 percent tax bracket. Work through your own situation a few times, and this should be easier to understand.

BASIC FEDERAL TAX ESTIMATOR

This is a guide only and is current as of 2018. It does not factor in child care, student loan interest deductions, medical expenses, moving expenses, and so on.

Gross Income (wages, interest income, etc.) $_____

Minus: **Adjustments** (IRA, 401(k), TSA, etc.) $_____

Equals: **Adjusted Gross Income** $_____

And the higher of:

Standard Deduction (Single: $12,000, Married: $24,000) $_____

Or

Itemized Deductions $_____
- State Income Tax
- Home Mortgage Interest and Property Taxes
- Charitable Contributions

Equals: **Taxable Income** $_____

Federal Income Tax Due (See tax table below): $_____

2018 INDIVIDUAL INCOME TAX RATES[14]

SINGLE				MARRIED FILING JOINTLY			
$0	to	$9,525	10%	$0	to	$19,050	10%
$9,525	to	$38,700	12%	$19,050	to	$77,400	12%
$38,700	to	$82,500	22%	$77,400	to	$165,000	22%
$82,500	to	$157,500	24%	$165,000	to	$315,000	24%
$157,500	to	$200,000	32%	$315,000	to	$400,000	32%
$200,000	to	$500,000	35%	$400,000	to	$600,000	35%
$500,000	to	No limit	37%	$600,000	to	No limit	37%

---

14. *2018 Tax Reference Guide*, Securian Financial Group.

WHAT DO YOU DO AT RETIREMENT?

Estimating your retirement needs is an important factor to consider at this stage of the pyramid. A financial-planning rule of thumb is to figure on needing 70 to 80 percent of your pre-retirement income, although more and more people are enjoying a retirement lifestyle that is close to what they enjoyed in their working years. This figure should be based on the income you plan to be earning at retirement, not the income you are making today. To estimate this amount, look at your current expenses and subtract the expenses and savings that you will not need at retirement. Add in extra expenses (e.g., travel, medical) that you might need. Consider the following:

- Will you still be paying a mortgage?
- Do you anticipate hefty medical expenses for yourself or your spouse?
- Do you wish to travel extensively?
- Will your day-to-day living expenses be similar to or less than what they are now?

If your budget allows and you have your Security and Confidence Stage taken care of, then take full advantage of any 401(k) or similar plans your employer offers, at least up until the amount the employer matches. This type of retirement investment defers tax payment on your contributed earnings until you withdraw the money, usually at retirement. If your employer matches any of your contribution, this is an added tax benefit.

UNIVERSAL RETIREMENT TRUTHS

Over the years, retirement planning has become increasingly complicated. To help simplify the process, here are four simple "truths" behind any advice we offer on retirement planning, no matter how complicated the specific issue.

Start Early

The sooner you begin contributing to your retirement plan, the more time your money has to compound. You can always make adjustments to keep your investment allocation on track with your risk-tolerance and time-horizon profile. However, if you delay getting started entirely, it is very difficult to catch up.

> The sooner you begin contributing to your retirement plan, the more time your money has to compound.

Diversify

With regard to your retirement plan, after you have determined an appropriate investment allocation for your contributions, make sure you understand the investment objectives of each individual fund you are investing in.

Two funds with different names might have very similar investment objectives, as well as holdings. Deferring investments in each fund will not give you the same degree of diversification as investing in two funds with different objectives.

We recommend that you work with a financial professional to determine an appropriate asset allocation for your retirement assets and to make sure you achieve a high level of diversification among the investment options.

Invest Consistently

Most plans allow you to make contributions on a payroll deduction basis. This allows you to make contributions to your investments every month. This eliminates any tendency to try to "time" the market. Over time, consistent investing can help you lower your investment costs.

> Regular investing over time is a method that "forces" you to buy more shares when the price of a fund is down and fewer when prices are higher.

Dollar cost averaging will produce a lower average cost per share compared to the average price per share over time. However, dollar cost averaging does not assure a profit and does not protect against loss in declining markets. Also, because such a program involves regular investment purchases regardless of fluctuating price levels of the investment, consider your financial ability to continue purchases through periods of low price levels.

Hang Tough

If your retirement is still fifteen, twenty, or even thirty years away, generally speaking, if you want the highest return potential, you should consider constructing a more aggressive investment allocation than that of an investment objective with a shorter time horizon. It is perfectly natural that such an investment allocation will experience higher levels of short-term fluctuation. This is necessary to potentially achieve a higher long-term rate of return.

> The time to worry about this is not during your peak earning years, when retirement is still many years away.

As you get closer to the time you will be drawing on this money, it will be necessary to begin shifting a greater percentage of your assets toward investments geared more toward capital preservation. The time to worry about this is not during your peak earning years, when retirement is still many years away. Ideally, at retirement, you will have multiple income sources and are withdrawing money from your qualified plans to "fill up" your 24 percent bracket and supplementing that with withdrawals from your non-qualified funds and cash value life insurance policies[15] for maximum tax leverage and efficiency. This is an area where the advice and wisdom of an experienced financial planner will be very valuable.

---

15. Life insurance products contain fees, such as mortality and expense charges, and can contain restrictions, such as surrender charges. Policy loans and withdrawals can create an adverse tax result in the event of a lapse or policy surrender and will reduce both the cash value and death benefit. Please keep in mind that the primary reason to purchase a life insurance product is the death benefit.

9

529 EDUCATION SAVINGS PLANS

There are various vehicles to assist in funding future education costs, but how much do you need to save? This can be a fairly tricky number to pin down if you have a young child and a lot of time before you will use the money.

There are a few trends to notice. For example, the average cost to attend all types of colleges seems to be rising higher than inflation rates, year after year. The cost of attending a four-year public university rose roughly 130 percent in the past decade. The average tuition was $14,499/year in 2005 and closed at an average of $19,189/year during the 2015–16 academic year. Private four-year schools in 2005 averaged $32,729. They, too, took a sizable jump, to an average of $39,529/year in 2015–16.[16]

Savingforcollege.com cites that the ten-year historical rate of increase as of 2011 for college tuition was 6 percent. If this rate were to continue into the future, the Rule of 72[17] would suggest that total costs could double every twelve years!

When it comes to planning for your children's future education costs, 529 savings plans can provide a great tax-advantaged investment opportunity for the high-income medical specialist. From an investment standpoint, such plans provide tax-deferred growth of earnings, extremely generous contribution limits, and currently tax-free distributions of investment gains for all qualified education expenses. (We'll expand on "qualified expenses" in a moment.)

It is our opinion that the features that make such plans so attractive have less to do with their tax treatment and more to do with issues of control and flexibility.

---

16. "Tuition Costs of Colleges and Universities," National Center for Education Statistics, https://nces.ed.gov/fastfacts/display.asp?id=76.

17. "Rule of 72," Investopedia, http://www.investopedia.com/terms/r/ruleof72.asp#axzz23ix6Y9NY.

Let's look at these plans from two different perspectives:

- Tax and investment features
- Control and flexibility features

TAX AND INVESTMENT FEATURES

For the high-income medical specialist, one frustrating aspect of investment planning from a tax perspective is that, when income increases beyond certain annual amounts, many investments that have attractive tax treatments become unavailable, such as with Roth IRAs, or annual contribution limits become more restrictive as income goes up, such as with 401(k) and 403(b) plans.

Neither of these is an issue with the 529 plan. All investment earnings on the plan grow 100 percent tax-deferred, and the contribution limits would rarely be restrictive for the purpose of funding a child's education. Previously, 529 plans were intended to fund college expenses. However, with the tax changes in 2018, these assets can also be used to fund qualified K–12 education expenses (if the state plan you're using allows it). This is a big opportunity for savers, especially if you intend to pay for private education for your children.

> With the tax changes in 2018, these assets can also be used to fund qualified K–12 education expenses (if the state plan you're using allows it).

Contributions

Contributions to 529 plans are generally not tax-deductible, although some states do have state tax benefits on contributions. However, contributions are considered gifts for federal and estate tax purposes. For the 2018 tax year, anyone may take advantage of the annual gift tax exclusion by contributing $15,000 per year ($30,000 for married couples) to any beneficiary. For financially independent physicians, there is a unique rule for 529 plans that allows for an individual to use five years' worth of the annual gift tax exclusion by contributing up to $75,000 ($150,000 for married couples) in one calendar year, assuming no other gifts have been made.

This is a very nice feature for high-net-worth specialists looking for ways to incorporate gifting strategies into their estate plans.

The limits imposed on 529 plans are, generally speaking, so high that it is difficult to envision a scenario in which it would become restrictive. The total limits outside the above discussed annual limits do vary a bit from state to state. They are in the neighborhood of $280,000 to $320,000 per beneficiary! Provided you get started early on planning for your children's or grandchildren's future education costs to take full advantage of the tax-deferred growth of investment earnings, these limits should not present a problem.

Distributions

Once you have contributed money to a 529 plan for the benefit of a child or grandchild, and the plan balance has grown significantly over the years, now it is time to begin withdrawing the money to pay for education expenses. So what happens? When you withdraw money from the account, it will be considered one of two things: a qualified distribution or a non-qualified distribution.

- Distributions that you use to pay for qualified expenses such as room, board, tuition, and certain expenses will be considered *qualified withdrawals*. Therefore, they are free of both federal and, currently, state income tax. For the physician with a long-time horizon and children bound for academic greatness (and the accompanying price tag), there is potential to build up and withdraw all investment gains free of tax!

- Distributions that you use for anything other than a qualified expense will be considered a *non-qualified distribution*. The investment earnings will be taxed as ordinary income for the beneficiary and are subject to a 10 percent penalty. Because we wrote this book with the high-income medical specialist in mind, we consider the potential of having investment earnings of a child's 529 plan— *potentially* taxed at the *child's* rate plus a penalty—a worthwhile risk to take.

> We consider the potential of having investment earnings of a child's 529 plan *potentially* taxed at the *child's* rate plus a penalty—a worthwhile risk to take.

CONTROL AND FLEXIBILITY FEATURES

The tax and investment features of IRC Section 529 plans are undeniably attractive and make such plans a very powerful financial tool for the high-income medical specialist. However, given the uncertainty of a young child's academic future, we often find reluctance among our clients to fund such vehicles for their children, who might or might not need the money. These uncertainties are very well addressed in 529 plans.

Now let's look at some of their benefits from a control and flexibility standpoint.

1. Who controls the account?

The account owner controls the account. If your child reaches the age of majority in your home state, the 529 plan balance does not become an asset of your child! You, as the account owner, control how and when distributions are to be made.

2. Who can contribute to the account?

Anyone may make contributions to the plan.

3. What happens if my child receives a scholarship or goes to a less expensive school?

Perhaps one of the most attractive features of 529 plans from a flexibility standpoint is the ability to change beneficiaries at any point.

However, to avoid triggering a penalty on investment earnings, the new beneficiary must be a family member of the previous beneficiary. The ability to move money in one designated 529 plan to another child's plan—should he or she not go to school, attend a less expensive school, receive a scholarship, or any other reason—is a unique feature that gives parents a great deal of flexibility.

4. What happens if I don't use the money for education?

If the money being withdrawn from a 529 plan is being used for anything other than a qualified education expense, the investment earnings will be taxed at the beneficiaries' tax rate, plus a 10 percent penalty on earnings. It is wise to avoid pulling money out of 529 plans for non-qualified expenses. However, because the earnings are taxed at the beneficiaries' rate, it is not too terrible because the account has grown completely tax-deferred!

5. Must the beneficiary go to school in the state in which I established the plan?

No. Currently, all states recognize other state-sponsored 529 plans. So all distributions for qualified expenses will be tax-exempt from both federal and state taxes.

FUNDING YOUR CHILD'S IRC SECTION 529 SAVINGS PLAN

With all the advantages of 529 plans, the obvious question becomes, "How do we fund a plan for our child?"

When determining how to take full advantage of such plans, there are several assumptions you can predict with a fairly high degree of accuracy. Such factors include:

- The year in which your child enters college (if your intent is college funding).
- How many years (four or five) of post-secondary education you wish to be able to fund.
- The percentage of the total cost you, as a parent, wish to be able to pay for.

There are also many more variables you must simply make a best estimate for. Here are a few of these factors:

- The rate of inflation for college costs. As mentioned, college costs have experienced significant levels of increase over the years and will likely continue to rise at a rate greater than the overall cost of living.
- The investment rate of return of the assets in the 529 plan
- Where your child will attend school

All these variables must be considered when determining how to fund your child's plan to arrive at the most important objective: having adequate funds available within the plan to be able to pay for the type of education, the length of education, and the location of the education you planned for.

Any outcome other than this will result in one of two scenarios:

- **Not enough money saved up in the 529 plan**—This will likely result in funds being withdrawn from other investment vehicles that have not grown tax-deferred and will likely not reap the tax benefits when withdrawn. Because qualified distributions will be tax-exempt from both state and federal taxes, investment gains from other sources will likely be subject to tax! As discussed earlier, this is where an overfunded variable life insurance policy can come in very handy. Please see chapter 6 for important information regarding life insurance.

- **Too much money saved up in the 529 plan**—The likely result of too much money in the plan will be excessive non-qualified distributions. While the earnings will be taxed at your child's rate—a lower rate—this is only in the event that you withdraw funds for the benefit of the beneficiary. Should the money *not* be withdrawn for the benefit of your child, all investment earnings will be taxed at *your* ordinary income rate, plus a 10 percent penalty!

Err on the conservative side—fund a 529 plan up to the amount that you anticipate costs to be and at a level you feel comfortable with.

Our conclusion is that 529 Education Savings Plans are excellent financial tools for the purpose of saving for future college or education costs. They are particularly attractive for high-income medical specialists, given their investment, tax, and flexibility features. Like all aspects of your financial planning, regular monitoring is critical. As your child's academic greatness (hopefully!) begins to materialize, adjusting the contributions to the plan accordingly will ensure that the many benefits can be maximized.

Your state of residence might offer state tax advantages to residents who participate in the in-state plan. You might miss out on certain state tax advantages if you choose another state's 529 plan. Any state-based benefits should be one of many appropriately weighted factors you consider in making an investment decision. You should consult your financial, tax, or other advisor to learn more about how state-based benefits (including any limitations) would apply to your specific circumstances.

You might also wish to contact your home state's 529 plan program administrator to learn more about the benefits that might be available to you by investing in the in-state plan.

A 529 plan is a tax-advantaged investment program designed to help pay for qualified education costs. Participation in a 529 plan does not guarantee that the contributions and investment returns will be adequate to cover higher-education expenses. Contributors to the plan assume all investment risk, including the potential for loss of principal and any penalties for non-educational withdrawals.

OTHER WAYS TO SAVE FOR EDUCATION

Uniform Transfer to Minors Act (UTMA)/Uniform Gift to Minors (UGMA)

Another popular savings tool for children is a UTMA or UGMA. Annual gift tax limits apply (currently a max of $15,000 from one person to another, so a set of parents or grandparents can transfer $30,000 to one individual gift tax-free). Although you can put almost any asset into a UTMA/UGMA, typically for college, you would invest in mutual funds, stocks, or ETFs (exchange traded funds).

The nice part of a UTMA/UGMA is that the money does not have to be earmarked for anything in particular, as long as withdrawals are used for the benefit of the beneficiary. Another upside to using these accounts is the tax benefits on the growth of the account. In 2018, the first $2,100 of investment income is tax-free as a result of the Tax Cuts and Jobs Act (TCJA). After that, it's taxed at "kiddie tax rates," which vary based on the size of the account. But be careful because it can get up to 37 percent.

Age of majority varies by state.

The potential downside of funding these accounts is that the child has complete control over these funds when he or she reaches the age of majority, which can range from eighteen to twenty-five, but most often age twenty-one. Age of majority varies by state. Check with your financial professional to determine if the minor has reached the age of majority in your state.

The main difference, potentially, between a UTMA and a UGMA is that the termination age can vary from state to state (commonly twenty-one for UTMA and eighteen for UGMA,) but please consult specific state legal guidelines.

Also, a UGMA can restrict the types of assets that transfer and can be slightly more restrictive on usage, which typically leads most advisors to lean toward the UTMA over the UGMA.

Coverdell ESA

Similar to a 529, the funds in the plan are allowed to grow tax-deferred and come out tax-free when used for qualified education expenses. A potential downside of these accounts is that the assets must be used by the age of thirty, and contributions must not be made past age eighteen. Unfortunately, you are also phased out of a Coverdell plan in a phased income range of MAGI from $190,000 to $220,000 for Married Filing Jointly, and contributions are limited up to $2,000/year. An upside to this plan is that you can use these savings to pay for K–12 expenses as well. Now that this is potentially doable with 529 plans, as of 2018 these are becoming more irrelevant.

Non-Qualified Brokerage Accounts

Of course, any savings are good savings at the end of the day, and you could always invest money in an independent brokerage account. This is an account that is in your name and that you have complete control over. You can choose your investments to be any stock, bond, or mutual fund out there, and you can manage the risk to suit your

tolerance and time horizon for use of the funds. The downside is that you will be subject to paying capital gains tax on any realized gains.

Grants/Scholarships

These are mechanisms for receiving aid that do not need to be paid back. Traditionally, grants are "needs-based," while scholarships are "merit-based," but this is not always the case. The world of options here is vast, and we recommend starting with exploring the educational institution's specific options.

> For resources outside the institution, you can look for assistance from the federal government, state government, and private and nonprofit organization.

Outside Loans

Many banks are now surfacing in this low-interest-rate environment outside traditional government lending. It is important, if you are seeking financing of tuition and expenses through loans, to comb through both private loan options and traditional government lending options.

The *Speculation Stage* involves risking money you can afford to lose. Some people are never comfortable with this and thus should not consider it; they should simply build their financial pyramid wider. This stage can involve different priorities for different people, such as buying very speculative individual stocks or aggressive specialty mutual funds.

Investing your money where the principal has a high degree of volatility and risk has potentially high returns, but you could also lose your money completely.

It is appropriate that this stage fits at the top of the pyramid because if the money is lost, it won't be devastating to your overall financial plan.

> Never invest more than one year's worth of net-worth growth!

Our rule of thumb when deciding how much to risk in a business opportunity or other aggressive venture is one year's worth of net-worth growth. Never invest more than this! In a worst-case scenario, if you lost the entire amount of your investment, you have basically lost one year's worth of financial progress. While not fun, it is not financially devastating. People get into trouble and can't recover financially when they gamble with a lifetime's worth of savings.

For example, let's say your net worth is $1 million, and conservatively projected a year from now, it will be $1,080,000. This growth would be from additional savings, reducing debts, and/or growth from your existing assets. In any event, the $80,000 projected growth is the absolute maximum amount that you should consider for a very speculative investment.

In the event that an opportunity has come along that requires more than this amount, do not be tempted to risk more. Consider lowering your investment, delaying the timing until your net worth has grown, or involving a financial professional.

Again, keep in mind that speculative investments, while valid financial tools, are typically used only by extremely savvy investors and/or high-net-worth investors and institutions. They are not recommended for anyone who cannot afford to lose a substantial amount of their net worth. These investments carry an extraordinary amount of risk and generally require intensive research and knowledge to carry out.

> Speculative investments, while valid financial tools, are typically used only by extremely savvy investors and/or high-net-worth investors and institutions.

In summary, very few physicians have ever gotten into trouble financially by being too conservative for too long. Sure, there are some potential lost-opportunity costs, but you can get into a lot of financial trouble by being too aggressive with too much money. That's why the financial pyramid is such a useful tool ; it helps you organize and prioritize these decisions.

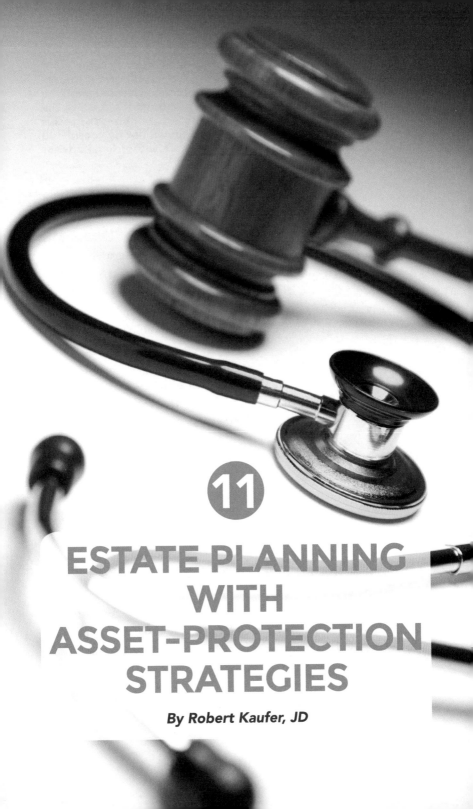

11

ESTATE PLANNING WITH ASSET-PROTECTION STRATEGIES

By Robert Kaufer, JD

Asset-protection planning should not be viewed as a strategy to avoid paying legitimate and reasonable creditors, but as a process to protect your personal assets from unreasonable creditors. "Unreasonable creditors" are those who bring frivolous lawsuits or get unreasonable jury awards related to medical malpractice or personal liability claims such as automobile or slip-and-fall accidents. These unreasonable creditors do exist. They are the predators looking to sue anyone who is successful. It could be any legal action for which a valid claim simply doesn't exist.

> In general, asset protection is about putting up barriers in front of the unreasonable creditors to make it difficult or impossible for them to get your personal and business assets.

Here are three key questions to ask yourself regarding asset protection:

1. What should I do?
2. When should I do it?
3. How far do I need to go?

1. WHAT SHOULD I DO?

The first step in navigating the asset-protection choices is to get educated. This chapter is not intended to be an exhaustive treatise on asset protection, but a primer to get you going in the right direction. It also is not intended to be legal advice and should not be taken as such. It is for information purposes only. Before implementing any asset-protection strategy, you should consult with an attorney licensed to practice law.

EXEMPT ASSETS

The first line of defense against unreasonable creditors is the protection you get from the state you live in. Each state, through its statutes, exempts certain assets from creditors. These assets can include all or a portion of the following:

- **Your home**—In many states, you get an exemption from creditors for your home. This, however, is usually not an unlimited exemption, and in some states (New Jersey, for example), there is no exemption at all. Other states (such as Florida) give an unlimited exemption, meaning a creditor cannot force you to sell your home to pay off a judgment, no matter what the value is. While these two states present both ends of the spectrum, most the states fall somewhere in between. An example is Minnesota, where the statute allows you to protect $390,000 of equity in your home. If the difference between your home's market value and all mortgages is greater than $390,000, a creditor can force you to sell your home and pay the creditor any amount over the exemption.

- **Life insurance**—Some states will protect life insurance partially or entirely. This can be both the cash value and/or the death benefit.

  o States such as Texas protect all the cash value paid into a life insurance contract. This means a creditor cannot force you to withdraw funds to pay off a debt.

  o In contrast to the laws of Texas, Minnesota protects the cash value only up to $4,000. Any amount above that can be reached by a creditor. Check with your local attorney to find out if this has changed.

- **Annuities**—Annuities are similar to life insurance. Each state decides how much, if any, can be protected from creditors.

- **IRAs**—State laws also give a certain amount of protection to individual retirement accounts, and the protection varies from state to state. Again, it can be all, nothing, or somewhere in between. The trend, however, is for greater protection to be given to these types of accounts. These laws are changing. In fact, Congress recently passed new bankruptcy legislation that included provisions for increased protection of traditional and Roth IRAs owned by a person in a bankruptcy proceeding.

- **ERISA-governed retirement plans**—These plans are most commonly employer-sponsored profit-sharing/401(k) plans. They are different from IRAs in that they are governed by federal law instead of state law. In most cases, federal law will trump state laws, including judgments that require that you liquidate an ERISA-governed plan to pay a creditor.

Contact an attorney licensed in your state to determine what protections your state will give you against the unreasonable creditor.

BASIC ESTATE PLANNING: WILLS OR REVOCABLE TRUSTS

The foundation for any asset-protection strategy is to have your basic estate plan in place. The two primary documents you can choose from for your basic estate plan are the will and the revocable living trust. While neither of these estate-planning documents gives much asset protection during your life, they can (if properly drafted) give good protection to your heirs.

Last Will and Testament

ARTICLE I: Funeral expen...

I direct my exec...

The Will

Having a will does not mean your estate can avoid probate. It is an instruction manual to the probate court on how your probate-eligible property should be distributed, who should do it, and, if your children are under the age of majority, who should be their guardian.

While you are alive, a will does nothing to give you asset protection because you continue to own your property in your name. It can give some asset protection to your heirs, depending on the complexity of the planning.

The probate process is designed to be a creditor's forum. Any known creditors must be given notice, and there is a waiting period for creditors to stake their claims.

The Revocable Living Trust

A revocable living trust is an alternative to using a will for your primary estate-planning documents. Having a properly funded revocable living trust will avoid probate, but it does not protect your assets from creditors. It can, however, if correctly drafted, give good asset protection for your heirs after your death.

The fact that the revocable living trust, if properly and completely funded, avoids the probate process and the creditor-friendly rules that come with it is reason enough to choose it over a will as your basic estate-planning vehicle.

FAMILY LIMITED LIABILITY COMPANIES AND FAMILY LIMITED PARTNERSHIPS

One of the more common strategies used in asset protection to build on basic estate planning is the (family) limited liability company (FLLC) or the (family) limited partnership (FLP).

FLLC

An LLC is a form of business entity that has become increasingly popular. It combines the liability protection of a cor-poration with the tax- and asset-protection advantages of a general partnership. All fifty states  have enacted LLC laws, with most of them looking and feeling like a general partnership. Some states (Minnesota, in particular) have taken on the feel of the corporation with two levels of management (governor and manager). This feature makes it ideal for the FLLC because it allows a husband and wife to maintain various levels of control over the company, depending on their life circumstances.

You can elect to have your LLC taxed like a corporation or a partnership. However, the majority of LLCs today are taxed like a partnership. That means the owners of these LLCs do not pay income tax. The income flows through directly to the members and is reported on their personal tax returns.

To begin the LLC, articles of organization are filed with the state in which you intend to set up the company. Some states (such as Minnesota) allow you to keep the names of the members, governors, and managers private and file only the name of the organizer (in most cases, the attorney who sets up the company). Having this anonymity can provide benefits and is an important component of an asset-protection strategy.

FLP

General Partnerships

A *general partnership* is formed when two or more persons agree to carry on a business together to make a profit. It is as simple as that. No writing has to be done, and no documents need to be filed with the state, except to register the name to be used. It is good practice, however, for any partnership to have a written partnership agreement so all partners understand their rights and responsibilities. The problem with a general partnership is that all partners are jointly and separately liable for all debts of the partnership. I recommend that you avoid a general partnership at all costs because of this liability trap. If a partnership is to be used in an asset-protection setting, it should be formed as a limited partnership.

> Avoid a general partnership at all costs because of this liability trap.

Limited Partnerships

A *limited partnership* consists of one or more general partners and one or more limited partners. A general partner handles the control and management of the partnership. The trade-off for this is that he or she has unlimited personal liability for all debts and obligations of the partnership. The limited partners cannot be involved in the control or management of the partnership, but they do enjoy protection from the debts of the partnership because their liability is limited to their investments in the entity. If limited partners do participate in the control or management of the partnership, they can lose their limited liability.

Choosing Between the Two

For many years, the FLP was the entity of choice for asset protection and the minimization of estate taxes. But since its advent, the LLC is fast becoming the entity of choice because it is more flexible than the FLP and because there is no unlimited liability for the general partners as there is with an FLP. In a family LLC, the husband and wife can be involved in the management of the company without losing their liability shield while there are no creditors. If a lawsuit arises, the spouse/defendant resigns from his or her management role but retains personal liability protection.

> The LLC is fast becoming the entity of choice because it is more flexible than the FLP.

Creditor Cannot Reach Assets of an FLP or FLLC

In most states, the only remedy for a judgment creditor of an LLC or a limited partnership is a "charging order," which is a legal remedy that gives the creditor the right to receive any distributions from an FLP or FLLC. It does not give the creditor the right to become an owner or to have a say in the management of the company. The creditor receives only the distributions intended to go to the owner/debtor. If this happens, the FLP/FLLC will simply choose not to make any distributions. The poison pill, however, is that even if the FLP/FLLC does not make a distribution, the creditor is responsible for the tax consequences, as if a distribution had been made, when the entity is taxed as a partnership.

> Great care must be put into the "operating agreement" to give the maximum protection possible from creditors.

The idea behind charging-order protection is simple enough: owners should not be involuntarily forced into a partnership with somebody they do not choose. To get complete protection from this strategy, however, great care must be put into the "operating agreement" to give the maximum protection possible from creditors. Using this entity to hold the assets you most want to protect allows you to protect them from creditors.

It's important to understand that you must adhere to the business formalities of whatever business structure you establish. The risk is that if you don't, you could lose asset-protection or estate-planning benefits. Please consult an attorney.

TRUSTS

Irrevocable Trusts

In planning, it is important to keep the revocable living trust concept separate from the irrevocable trust. The revocable living trust can be amended or revoked (you retain complete control as long as you are alive and competent), but it gives limited asset protection. On the other hand, the irrevocable trust will protect your assets (assuming the transfer of property was not a fraudulent conveyance), but you lose all control and benefit. In a properly executed asset-protection strategy, trusts play an important role.

One of the more common uses is to own life insurance. If the trust is created properly and all the administrative formalities are followed, it will keep the proceeds out of a deceased person's estate for tax purposes and keep them away from creditors.

Asset-Protection Trusts

A strategy that is gaining popularity is the *asset protection trust* (APT). An APT is a self-settled trust, meaning it is funded by the creator of the trust, who is also the beneficiary. This is different from the irrevocable trust discussed above because in a traditional irrevocable trust, the intended beneficiary is usually the spouse or children, not the person who creates the trust.

> An APT is funded by the creator of the trust, who is also the beneficiary.

There are two main types of APTs: the domestic APT and the offshore (foreign) APT.

A. Domestic APT

In many states, a *self-settled APT* is not allowed. But in a minority of states, recent legislation is beginning to allow such asset-protection vehicles. Eight states (Alaska, Delaware, Rhode Island, Missouri, Utah, Oklahoma, South Dakota, and Nevada) now allow some form of a self-settled trust to be set up that is outside the reach of creditors. These are very new and have yet to be challenged in court. Many legal scholars

believe they are unconstitutional because of the "Full Faith and Credit" clause of the Constitution, which says, "A state is to recognize the judgment from another state." This sets up a conflict-of-state-laws issue (the self-settled APT is exempt from judgment creditors in the state it was created) and the Constitution. This means the creditor must simply register the judgment and does not have to initiate the lawsuit all over again in that state.

B. Offshore APT

An *offshore* or *foreign APT* is similar to a domestic APT except that the trust situs (location) is in a foreign jurisdiction. The Cook Islands or Nevis are two popular destinations. These trusts are self-settled, but the trustee is located in one of these foreign jurisdictions, thereby putting him or her out of reach of the US courts. Creditors would not simply be able to register a US judgment in one of these jurisdictions. They would have to initiate a new lawsuit.

> While the trustee and trust may be outside the reach of the US courts, the creator of the trust is not unless he or she leaves the country.

Many state and federal judges despise this set-up and will do whatever is in their power to unwind this type of trust, including putting the creator of the trust in jail for contempt of court. There is a long line of cases that deal with this issue, many not favorable to the debtor. These trusts are very expensive to set up and administer, and they should probably be used only in extreme cases and not with all assets. Consult with an expert asset-protection attorney before considering these trusts.

2. WHEN SHOULD I DO IT?

Use time as your ally. Having a plan in place and implemented for a period of time before an event (judgment or death) occurs will give the plan a better chance of withstanding an attack by a creditor or the IRS. If you wait until a lawsuit is initiated or even after an event occurs that might cause a lawsuit to be initiated, it might be too late because any transfer may be deemed a "fraudulent conveyance." That scenario will likely quash any asset-protection strategies you implement, on the theory that its only purpose was to deny creditors their claims.

3. HOW FAR DO I NEED TO GO?

Assess your risk by the cost of implementing an asset-protection plan, and take the action that gives you the protection you're comfortable with. With that in mind, here are some planning rules of thumb.

PLANNING RULES OF THUMB

The following guidelines can help you de-ciding if you need asset-protection planning. However, the final decisions must weigh the risk of a lawsuit with the cost of the protection. In many cases, the tools referenced in this chapter make good sense for successful individuals, no matter the stage of their careers.

> Weigh the risk of a lawsuit with the cost of the protection.

1. **If you do not have children**—You might not need to undertake any estate planning at this time, but you should consult with an attorney in your area to make the final decision.

2. **If you have children**—You need to take some action to get the bare minimum for estate planning. You should be considering guardians for custody of your children and trustees to handle their finances if both parents die. If asset protection concerns or will concern you, it is best to begin with revocable trusts.

Another option is to use testamentary trusts inside your will. Keep in mind that these techniques alone do not provide asset protection for you, although they can provide protection to your heirs. These options are more expensive than basic wills, but it will be money well spent because they will be the foundation of your overall plan.

3. **If you are early in your career**—If you are just starting out, you most likely will have a low net worth and high debt load. Even though your net worth is relatively low, you should consider enlisting an attorney to help you decide whether wills or revocable trusts with pour-over wills are appropriate for your main estate-planning tools.

4. **If you own a business or professional practice**—If you have developed a successful business or professional practice and asset protection concerns you, you should look to implement the following procedures if your state-given exemptions do not give you the protection you want and need:

   a. If you have substantial after-tax investments, including cash value life insurance, annuities, rental real estate, or recreational property, you should consider an FLLC.

   b. If you have an FLLC, use it for your cash value life insurance. Then you could use a separate irrevocable life insurance trust for your term insurance, with total death benefits greater than $1.5 million to avoid estate taxes and protect the death benefits for your heirs.

CONCLUSION

If your intended goal of asset protection is to be completely judgment-proof, successful asset protection becomes extremely difficult. However, if your goal is to protect a portion of your estate against unreasonable creditors, that goal can be obtained with the help of an experienced financial planner and attorney. Without successful asset-protection planning, you will lose all assets that are not exempt if a judgment is awarded against you. With the right planning, you will be able to build walls between you and your creditors that will improve your bargaining position and help you protect what you have worked so hard to earn.

Remember, you need to take action before there are any potential lawsuits against you. Otherwise, the courts could unravel your actions.

As with every aspect of a financial plan, the estate-planning and asset-protection components are extensive and need to be coordinated by a professional advisor. Your advisor should obviously be very knowledgeable and should listen to you and your goals and then communicate your options…so you can work together.

Please keep in mind that the primary reason to purchase a life insurance product is the death benefit. Life insurance products contain fees, such as mortality and expense charges, and can contain restrictions, such as surrender periods. Policy loans and withdrawals can create an adverse tax result in the event of a lapse or policy surrender and will reduce both the cash value and death benefit.

12

CASE STUDIES

In this chapter, we provide five specific case studies that demonstrate the concepts outlined in this book. These will show that you can use the pyramid of financial needs in most circumstances as a method of organizing and prioritizing financial decisions. Of course, much of this process is subjective, and ultimately the correct answer merges the quantitative and qualitative aspects of the decision into a financial plan you are comfortable with. We hope you find the following case studies to be a helpful addition to the understanding of the techniques presented earlier in this book.

The following case studies are fictitious, and any similarities to any actual person(s) or situation(s) are coincidental. Please see the end of this chapter for important disclosure information regarding the financial products discussed.

CASE STUDY #1: FINISHING MEDICAL SCHOOL AND BEGINNING PGY1 YEAR

Kelli is single and finishing medical school. She will graduate in the spring and do a three-year emergency medicine residency.

She has a few financial goals at this time:

- Develop a budget to manage the new residency salary.
- Understand and sign up for appropriate employee benefits.
- Consider purchasing a home or condo.
- Understand and manage her student loan debt.
- Have a plan for emergencies and unexpected events.

The Numbers

Kelli will be living on $52,000/year, or approximately $3,150/month take-home pay. Even though her parents offered to loan her money for a down payment on a condo, she decided to rent an apartment because she will be in that town for only three years before moving somewhere else to continue her career.

Kelli's Net-Worth Statement

Fixed Assets:

Savings Account	$3,000
Checking Account	$1,000
Money Market Account	$0
Total Fixed Assets	**$4,000**

Variable Assets:

Roth IRA	$0
Mutual Funds	$0
403(b) Balance	$0
Total Variable Assets:	**$0**

Personal and Other Assets

Vehicle	$2,500
Personal Property	$3,000
Total	**$5,500**

Total Assets	**$9,500**

Liabilities:

Credit Cards (21%)	$2,300
Student Loans (6.8%)	$110,000
Total Liabilities	**$112,300**

Net Worth (Assets Minus Liabilities)	**($102,800)**

The Financial Plan

The following are our recommendations for Kelli at the four different stages of her financial-planning process.

1. Security and Confidence Stage

- Set up a money market mutual fund or high-interest savings account to use as her emergency reserve instead of the savings account.

- Immediately begin aggressively paying off the credit card debt with most of her extra monthly surplus cash flow.

- Secure a private individual disability policy to insure her greatest asset: her ability to earn an income. This policy should protect her in her "own occupation," include a cost of living feature, and include the maximum future purchase option, allowing her to increase the coverage later without medical underwriting.

- Because Kelli is planning on joining a private-practice EM group, she knows that she will not qualify for Public Service Loan Forgiveness. For that reason, she will look to refinance her student loans to secure the lowest interest rate possible after her grace period expires.

- Because she eventually wants to start a family, she will secure an inexpensive term life insurance policy with conversion features.

- Adding an umbrella liability policy is also a wise asset-protection strategy at this stage.

2. Capital Accumulation Stage

- Start a monthly savings program that includes putting money into a Roth IRA. The main objective here is just to get started and learn how to track these accounts online to increase her knowledge and confidence level.

3. Tax-Advantaged Stage

- Because Kelli is at the lowest income (and tax bracket) of her career, and there is no employer match on the 403(b) account, she should wait to contribute to a pre-tax retirement account.

4. Speculation Stage

- Wait until the rest of the pyramid is more established.

Summary

Kelli is normally a saver. She looks forward to beginning her training so she can start earning an income, which will allow her to pay off her credit cards and begin building a savings and investment plan. She is happy that she has started educating herself, building the base of her financial plan, and developing a trusting relationship with a financial planner.

CASE STUDY #2: SECOND YEAR OF RESIDENCY

Rupa is in her second year of an Ob/Gyn residency. Her husband, Rakesh, just finished graduate school and landed his first full-time job as a software engineer. They have no children.

Their financial goals and concerns are as follows:

- Pay off debt.
- Accumulate savings.
- Buy a starter home.
- Start a family.
- Begin retirement savings.
- Protect themselves against loss.

The Numbers

Rupa's income is $52,500 per year. Rakesh earns $65,000. They have $155,000 in student loans currently in forbearance at 6.8 percent interest. They have $3,000 in credit card debt, $4,000 in savings, and few other assets and debts. Their take-home pay is $7,000 per month, and they currently have about $3,000 per month in discretionary income. Their current rent payment is $1,300 per month.

Rupa and Rakesh's Net-Worth Statement

Fixed Assets:

Savings Account	$4,000
Checking Account	$2,000
Total Fixed Assets	**$6,000**

Variable Assets:

Roth IRAs	$3,000
403(b) Balance	$4,100
Total Variable Assets	**$7,100**

Personal and Other Assets:

Vehicles	$10,000
Personal Property	$11,000
Total	**$21,000**

Total Assets   **$34,100**

Liabilities:

Vehicle Loan (3%)	$10,000
Credit Cards (18%)	$3,000
Student Loans (6.8%)	$155,000
Total Liabilities	**$168,000**

Net Worth (Assets Minus Liabilities)   **($133,900)**

The Financial Plan

The following are our recommendations for Rupa at the four different stages of her financial-planning process.

1. Security and Confidence Stage

- Apply the majority of the surplus dollars toward eliminating the credit card debt, and once paid off, put that money into a money market mutual fund for emergencies and additional liquidity.

- Because Rupa does not like the outlook of Public Service Loan Forgiveness with her career, she should look to refinance her student loans to lower the interest rate. If possible, she should pay at least $2,500/year of interest to maximize the tax deduction because their income is less than $120,000.

- Obtain a private "own occupation" disability insurance policy with the maximum future-purchase option.

- Obtain inexpensive convertible term life insurance for both Rupa and Rakesh.

- Have a will drafted, including health care directives.

- Increase their emergency reserve fund once the credit cards are paid off.

- Purchase a $1 million umbrella liability policy if/when they purchase a home.

2. Capital Accumulation Stage

- Survey the real estate market for affordability, and start looking into areas of the city to purchase a home. Because they will most likely stay in the area when Rupa finishes residency, they would like to get a small starter home or condo and take advantage of current low interest rates.

- Determine the mortgage payment that is equivalent to their current rent payment. Due to the deductibility of mortgage interest and property taxes, it can be a big difference. In their case, the equivalent mortgage payment is $1,500, which would buy roughly a $250,000 home, including taxes if financed at 4.5 percent and amortized over thirty years.

- Purchase a home or condo for around $250,000 if suitable housing can be found in that price range using a physician mortgage option with a down payment of zero to 5 percent.

3. Tax-Advantaged Stage

- Begin Roth IRA contributions once the credit cards are paid off and an emergency reserve has been established.

- Contribute 6 percent of Rakesh's income to his 401(k) to take full advantage of the 3 percent employer match.

4. Speculation Stage

- Wait until the rest of the pyramid is more established.

Summary

This plan addresses current as well as future issues. The emphasis is placed on the Security and Confidence Stage by eliminating the credit cards, building an emergency fund, locking in life and disability insurance, and addressing their housing situation. Because the cost is relatively small, Rupa's future income has been protected with the addition of a properly structured disability policy that allows her to add coverage when she enters private practice. The term life insurance policy guarantees life insurance coverage will be in place when Rupa and Rakesh start a family. The umbrella liability policy is their first asset-protection component to better protect their personal assets from liability. The Roth IRA and 401(k) serve as building blocks to their investing and retirement needs.

CASE STUDY # 3: FINISHING RESIDENCY AND HEADING INTO FELLOWSHIP

George is in the final year of his orthopedic surgery residency and preparing for fellowship in a different state. He is single but expects to be married in one to two years, with children to follow soon after. George owns a small home that he purchased at the beginning of his residency, which he is selling. He plans to rent during the fellowship. Other than his mortgage, George has no other debt. His parents paid for his undergraduate and medical school. George has contributed the maximum annual contribution to his Roth IRA since he started residency and maintains a high balance in his checking account.

George's financial goals and concerns are as follows:

- Invest the profit from sale of his home.
- Get married and start a family in two years.
- Protect himself from future catastrophes.

The Numbers

George's current salary is $55,000 per year; however, in two months, his salary will be $57,000. His take-home pay in two months will be $3,475 per month. After expenses are paid, he should have $1,000 per month of surplus cash flow available.

George's Net-Worth Statement:

Fixed Assets:

Checking Account	$11,000
Total Fixed Assets	**$11,000**

Variable Assets:

Roth IRA	$22,000
403(b)	$0
Total Variable Assets	**$22,000**

Personal and Other Assets:

Home	$142,000
Vehicle	$5,000
Personal Property	$2,000
Total	**$149,000**

Total Assets	**$182,000**

Liabilities:

Mortgage (4.25%)	$129,000
Total Liabilities	**$129,000**

Net Worth (Assets Minus Liabilities)	**$53,000**

The Financial Plan

The following are our recommendations for George at the four different stages of his financial-planning process.

1. Security and Confidence Stage

- Maintain an emergency fund such as a savings account, interest-bearing checking account, or money market for funds currently held in a non-interest-bearing checking account. The balance of the cash-flow surplus, after acquiring the necessary insurance programs noted below, should be committed to the same account for future expenses such as the wedding and moving expenses.

- Obtain two individual disability policies with a maximum future-purchase option. Because each company limits total future coverage, obtaining two separate policies with two separate companies will allow George to protect himself to the fullest extent because he anticipates an income as a hand surgeon of more than $500,000/year a few years into private practice.

- Obtain inexpensive convertible term life insurance.

- Purchase a $1 million liability umbrella policy.

- If he has a hard time selling his home, consider renting to an incoming resident in his department and refinancing to a fixed interest rate mortgage.

2. Capital Accumulation Stage

- Upon the sale of his home, deposit the proceeds in a secure interest-bearing account, such as a savings account, or in a money market. Funds will then be readily available to use for upcoming expenses.

3. Tax-Advantaged Stage

- Continue maximum Roth IRA contributions in the current year, and in the subsequent year, if George's combined income from a partial-year fellowship and partial year in practice does not exceed the IRS income limits.

- Transfer the current Roth IRA to an efficiently managed investment platform instead of the bank money market where it is currently invested. Because this is long-term money, George's underlying investments should be more growth-oriented using stocks and stock mutual funds.

- With additional cash flow, start contributing to the 403(b) offered through his fellowship. While there is no matching in this plan, there is a Roth 403(b) option that allows him to save more post-tax dollars while he is in one of the lowest tax brackets he will ever be in.

4. Speculation Stage

- Wait until the base of the financial pyramid is more established.

Summary

At this stage of George's career, his plan focuses on the importance of the Security and Confidence Stage, strengthening the foundation, or base, of the pyramid. Emphasis is placed on building a solid foundation for the future by maintaining sufficient liquidity for future expenses and obtaining individual life and disability insurance to protect him and his future family's income. With minimal cost, George has protected current and future income through the purchase of an occupation-specific disability policy with a future-purchase-option rider that allows him to add significant coverage once he is in practice, without providing evidence of insurability. The term life insurance he acquires when he is insurable will provide immediate protection for when he starts a family. The liability umbrella is a foundational asset protection component. The Roth IRA and 403(b) are fundamental to his retirement needs.

CASE STUDY # 4: DUAL-PHYSICIAN COUPLE FIVE YEARS INTO PRACTICE

Adam finished his plastic surgery residency five years ago and has been working hard to pay off debt and get established in his practice, while balancing time with his family. He was recently given the opportunity to buy into the practice and plans on this happening in the next month or two. His wife, Natalie, a radiation oncologist, has been home part time with their child for the past four and a half years. The plan is for her to work full time when their son, Evan, starts kindergarten in the fall.

They have many financial goals at this time:

- Build the house of their dreams in a few years.
- Buy into Adam's practice and become a partner.

- Continue to pay off their debts.
- Start to save for Evan's college.
- Save for retirement.
- Reduce tax liability.
- Establish wealth/asset protection.
- Have a plan for emergencies and unexpected events.

The Numbers

Adam works in a midsized clinic as a cosmeticc surgeon with an annual income of $350,000. Once he becomes a partner, his annual income will increase to at least $600,000 to 700,000. He has to pay for his own benefits, such as health insurance, disability insurance, life and malpractice insurance, and his own retirement plan. His disability policy is adequate for his current income, but it would be insufficient coverage for the income he would be stepping into as a partner. He recently purchased a $500,000 term life insurance policy to cover the cost of the mortgage in the event of his death.

Natalie works part time in a radiation oncology practice with an annual income of $150,000. Once she starts working full time in the fall, her annual income will increase to $320,000. She also has to provide her own insurance coverage, but unlike Adam, her employer has a qualified retirement plan that allows her to defer up to $18,500 of her income per year. The only life and disability coverage she owns are the small policies she purchased during residency five years ago.

In the next four months, their monthly take-home pay will increase to $38,000, and their monthly expenses will increase to $20,000 (which includes the business loan repayment for Adam's buy-in), leaving $18,000 per month in excess funds with which to plan.

Natalie and Adam's Net-Worth Statement

Fixed Assets:

Savings Account	$75,000
Checking Account	$23,000
Total Fixed Assets	**$98,000**

Variable Assets:

IRA	$13,000
Roth IRA	$9,000
Mutual Funds	$249,000
Individual Stocks	$42,000
Total Variable Assets	**$313,000**

Personal and Other Assets:

Home	$675,000
Vehicles	$60,000
Personal Property	$40,000
Medical Practice (assuming Adam buys in)	$1,000,000
Total	**$1,775,000**

Total Assets	**$2,186,000**

Liabilities:

Mortgage (30-year at 6%)	$510,000
Home Equity Line (7%)	$25,000
Vehicle Loan (4%)	$40,000
Student Loans (3.5%)	$150,000
Medical Practice Loan (7%)	$1,000,000
Total Liabilities	**$1,725,000**

Net Worth (Assets Minus Liabilities)	**$461,000**

The Financial Plan

The following are our recommendations for Adam and Natalie at the four different stages of their financial-planning process.

1. Security and Confidence Stage

- Increase their umbrella liability insurance to $4 million.

- Maximize uninsured/underinsured auto coverage.

- Secure an additional personal disability policy on both Adam and Natalie to supplement their current policies, which are inadequate for their income-to-be.

- Secure $5 million of life insurance on Adam and $3 million on Natalie, using a majority of term insurance and a small (appropriately structured and funded) permanent policy.

- Increase their home equity line of credit to be used for emergencies.

- Start contributing an additional $2,000 toward debts because the allocation of additional funds should accomplish their financial goals (see below).

- Draft wills, trusts, and appropriate estate-planning documents.[18]

2. Capital Accumulation Stage

- The balance of the cash-flow surplus, after making improvements in the insurance noted above and debt reduction, should be committed to the following savings programs:

  o Initiate a 529 plan for Evan's college and fund it at $1,500 per month. They do not have a state tax deduction.

  o Initiate a brokerage account and build a portfolio of non-qualified mutual funds ($10,000 per month).

  o Fund permanent cash value life policies up to the limits allowed that do not turn the policies into modified endowment contracts (MEC's) at $1,500 per month. Not only do these policies have some tax advantages, but Adam and Natalie worked with their attorney and learned that the policies are also exempt from creditors

---

18. Find a qualified attorney to draft documents, and make sure you understand all terms and conditions of any arrangements. Financial advisors do not provide tax or legal advice.

in their state. That provides them significant asset protection.

    o   Consider building their dream house sooner rather than later to take advantage of today's lower interest rates and to allow enjoyment of the house with the family for many more years.

3. Tax-Advantaged Stage

- Adam and his partners contribute $49,000 to a self-directed retirement account. They each have a fee-based account using load-waived mutual funds. Adam chose an aggressive growth portfolio that is broadly diversified across all sectors; he needs to monitor it quarterly with his financial advisors.

- Continue to maximize the contribution into Natalie's 401(k) retirement plan ($18,500 per year). Make sure this is managed using a carefully constructed growth-style portfolio.

4. Speculation Stage

- They are not comfortable using any of their funds for speculative investing at this time and have decided to continue to build the "base" of the pyramid, as described earlier. At some point, they would like to pursue some riskier investments, which would fit into this stage.

Summary

With newly added risk-management vehicles such as the increased life, disability, and umbrella liability insurances, Adam and Natalie's new plan is firmly anchored. They are happy knowing that their estate plan is in good order and can adapt as their family and financial wealth grow. In addition, they are now able to adapt to their increasing income by properly allocating their short-, mid-, and long-term savings. And last, they have started to work with an architect to build their dream home and can pursue that goal sooner than they imagined. They can't believe how fast all these changes have taken place but are relieved to have an efficient plan that can keep up with their very busy lives.

CASE STUDY #5: MID-CAREER JOB CHANGE

Anne and Tom are both in their mid-forties and have three children, ages sixteen, fifteen, and eleven. Anne has worked as a pediatrician at a large teaching hospital since finishing her residency from the same institution. Tom is beginning to get back into consulting but still finds himself quite busy running the household, taking care of all the finances, and attending all the various activities the kids are in. He figures that any income will be offset by his expenses. But as the kids get older and enter college, he will be able to build up his business with the goal of making enough money to cover some of the kids' college expenses.

Recently, Anne was approached by a fast-growing multi-specialty group that is competing with the teaching hospital. She has been offered a significant signing bonus, a very competitive benefits package, and a three-year income guarantee. She is torn between being loyal to her existing partners and patients and taking the opportunity to increase her income significantly while working a more manageable schedule. She has become increasingly disappointed with the current teaching hospital and all the "politics." She states, "I just want to practice medicine."

Their primary financial goals include the following:

- Having Anne take a more active role in the financial-planning process.

- Determining what amount needs to be saved for each child to pay for 75 percent of college tuition and related expenses.

- Reviewing life and disability insurance for both of them.

- Analyzing their current retirement plan, which includes a defined benefit pension and a money purchase pension with the ability to contribute to a 403(b), and a 457 deferred compensation plan, to the retirement package Anne is being offered through the recruiting employer.

- Determine if their investment mix is in line with their investment objectives and risk tolerance and if the amount they are saving for retirement is sufficient.

- Maintain a greater amount of cash surplus available for planned and unanticipated expenses like family vacations, auto purchases and repairs, and home improvements.

The Numbers

Anne's current annual income is $185,000. The offer from the new employer is guaranteed at $215,000, plus a signing bonus to be negotiated. While not guaranteed forever, she believes the new clinic is dedicated to growing. Although she would miss the responsibilities of teaching younger residents, it is hard to pass up $30,000/year of increased income.

Anne and Tom's financial plan focuses on reviewing all the insurance and retirement plans being offered through Anne's current and potential new employer. An emphasis is on comparing the complex retirement options through both employers. While the retirement options are different in structure, the new employer offers a substantial match and a contribution to each physician's retirement account. This makes up for the fact that the teaching hospital has a defined benefit pension contribution that Anne would be walking away from.

Anne and Tom's Net-Worth Statement

Fixed Assets:

Savings Account	$4,500
Checking Account	$2,200
Money Market Account	$8,800
Total Fixed Assets	**$15,500**

Variable Assets:

Non-Qualified Jointly Held Brokerage Account	$58,000
Individual Stocks	$29,000
Anne's Retirement Plan from Former Employer	$287,000
Tom's 401(k) and IRA Rollover	$218,000
Total Variable Assets	**$592,000**

Personal and Other Assets:

Home	$850,000
Vehicles	$52,000
Personal Property	$38,000
Total	**$940,000**

Total Assets	**$1,547,500**

Liabilities

Mortgage (30-year at 6%)	$580,000
Vehicle Loan	$24,000
Credit Card	$600
Total Liabilities	**$604,600**

Net Worth (Assets Minus Liabilities)	**$942,900**

The Financial Plan

The following are our recommendations for Anne and Tom at the four different stages of their financial-planning process.

1. Security and Confidence Stage

- Split the majority of the signing bonus between a money market mutual fund and a very conservative mutual fund to increase their emergency reserves to a more appropriate level.

- Refinance their mortgage to a new thirty-year fixed rate at about 4 percent. They could do a fifteen-year mortgage but would rather stretch the mortgage out so they can put more money toward the kids' college education funds. The 2 percent savings on their $580,000 mortgage will save more than $11,000/year in interest.

- In reviewing their life and disability insurance, Anne owns a $1 million twenty-year term policy that she purchased fifteen years ago. In addition, she has almost $600,000 of group life insurance at her current employer. Anne also owns a disability policy with a $3,000 monthly benefit. The only life insurance on Tom is the spousal benefit of $50,000 through Anne's employer. After a "needs analysis" that quantifies the amount of coverage someone needs, Anne should have $2,200,000 of coverage, and Tom should have $500,000.

- We recommend that Anne increase her personal insurance to $2 million and to supplement it with another $200,000 through work. This life insurance protection should be made up of term insurance. The term policy will allow them to stretch the amount of insurance they have, given the dollars they are allocating from their cash flow. Tom currently does not own life insurance but should own at least $500,000 of term coverage. In the event of Tom's premature death, Anne would be able to work a 60 percent schedule to spend more time with the kids during their teenage years.

2. Capital Accumulation Stage

- In addition to saving for retirement, Anne and Tom will be adding to their brokerage account, when possible, for future major expenditures such as a possible vacation home, remodeling project, and other larger financial expenses for the children.

- Along with the supplemental retirement savings, Tom and Anne should transfer the stocks to their existing brokerage account.

- Because they hope to fund 75 percent of their children's college expenses, they need to invest a total of $1,200 monthly into a 529 plan for each of the three children. They should invest the remaining 40 percent, or $600 per month, into the brokerage account in mutual funds the parents will own. Tom and Anne assume that college expenses will be in the $30,000-per-year range, which we assume would increase at a rate of 5 percent per year.

3. Tax-Advantaged Stage

- We advise Anne to roll over her retirement plan into an IRA. When deciding what allocation is appropriate for her account, we also need to consider the investment choices within the new retirement plans so all of these long-term dollars work together.

- After reviewing the retirement analysis, we determined that, in addition to Anne contributing the maximum to her 401(k) plan, she and Tom should also be saving monthly. An automatic monthly savings plan will be established that will be invested into Tom and Anne's non-qualified brokerage account.

4. Speculation Stage

- Wait until the rest of the pyramid is more established.

Summary

Anne and Tom are now on a path toward accomplishing their financial goals—college for their children and their own retirement—while doing an excellent job of managing their year-to-year expenditures. They are taking advantage of tax-preferred items such as 529 plans and the 401(k) plan. In the event of a death, disability, or illness, they have properly protected their family financially. This investment plan will allow them to build for future expenses, and the cash account in the money market should provide them with funds to do the things they enjoy doing with their family, without the need to go into debt or create a problem when unexpected expenses occur. They enjoy having better control of Anne's investment choices with her IRA rollover versus having the funds in her prior employer's 401(k). She also finds work more enjoyable knowing that "there is a light at the end of the tunnel" and knowing that her hard work is helping them achieve their financial goals. They will continue to meet with their financial advisor to monitor this financial and life plan together.

Variable life insurance and mutual funds are sold only by prospectus. The prospectus contains important information about the product's investment objectives, charges, and expenses, as well as the risks and other information associated with the product. You may obtain a copy of the prospectus from your representative. You should carefully consider the risks and investment charges of a specific product before investing. You should always read the prospectus carefully before investing. Investments in a money market fund are neither insured nor guaranteed by the FDIC or any government agency. Although the fund seeks to preserve the value of your investment at $1.00 per share, it is possible to lose money by investing in the fund.

Life insurance products contain fees, such as mortality and expense charges, and may contain restrictions, such as surrender charges. Policy loans and withdrawals can create an adverse tax result in the event of a lapse or policy surrender and will reduce both the cash value and death benefit. If a policy is overfunded and becomes a modified endowment contract (MEC), the contract's earnings will be taxed as ordinary income at withdrawal and might be subject to a 10 percent penalty if withdrawn before age 59½. Please keep in mind that the primary reason to purchase a life insurance product is the death benefit.

A 529 education savings plan is a tax-advantaged investment program designed to help pay for qualified higher-education costs. Participation in a 529 plan does not guarantee that the contributions and investment returns will be adequate to cover higher-education expenses. Contributors to the plan assume all investment risk, including the potential for loss of principal, and any penalties for non-educational withdrawals. Your state of residence might offer state tax advantages to residents who participate in the in-state plan, subject to meeting certain conditions or requirements. You could miss out on certain state tax advantages should you choose another state's 529 plan. Any state-based benefits should be one of many appropriately weighted factors to be considered in making an investment decision. You should consult with your financial, tax, or other advisor to learn more about how state-based benefits (including any limitations) would apply to your specific circumstances. You might also wish to contact your home state's 529 plan Program Administrator to learn more about the benefits that might be available to you by investing in the in-state plan.

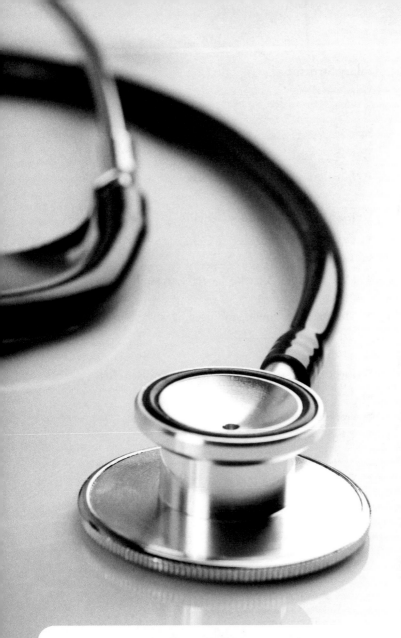

APPENDIX

EMPLOYEE BENEFITS CHECKLIST
FOR THE PHYSICIAN

☐ **Salary Structure**

    Year 1: _____

    Year 2: _____

    Year 3: _____

    Year 4: _____

    Year 5: _____

☐ **Major Medical Insurance Benefits**

- Deductible _____
- Top limits _____
- Hospitalization benefits for self and family (describe) _____
  _____
- Medical and dental reimbursement programs
  Top limit _____

☐ **Group Long-Term Disability Insurance Benefits**

- Amount _____
- Premiums paid by:
  Self: _____
  Corporation: _____
- Wage continuation program if disabled (describe) _____
  _____
- Short-term disability insurance (describe)
  _____

☐ **Group Life Insurance Benefits**

- Face amount while in practice

  _____

- Face amount after retirement

  _____

☐ **Pension/Profit-Sharing Plan Benefits**

- What are the eligibility requirements?

  _____

- Where are the funds invested?

  _____

- What is the formula?

  _____

- What is the vesting schedule?

  _____

- What does the most recent actuarial valuation show past service liability to be?

  _____

- What is the availability of voluntary contribution under the plan?

  _____

☐ **Malpractice Insurance**
- Who pays the premiums? _____
- Umbrella coverage _____
- Amount of coverage _____
- Claims made or occurrence policy

  _____

☐ **Automobile Reimbursement**
- Auto _____
- Repairs _____
- Gas _____

☐ **Vacation Policy**
- How are vacation times determined?

  _____

- Amount of vacation time available

  _____

- Compensation arrangements if more time is taken _____

  _____

☐ **Reimbursement for Continuing Education**
- Reimbursement for attendance at conferences

  _____

- Reimbursement for professional affiliation dues, subscriptions _____
- Reimbursement for time off used to prepare for Boards ___
_____

☐ **Does the firm arrange for a line of credit for the new physician?** _____

☐ **Are there any privileges restricted to senior physicians?** _____

☐ **Are any extra duties expected of the new physician that are not performed by senior physicians?**
- Evening calls _____
- Weekend calls _____
- Other _____

☐ **Is the new physician invited to all corporation meetings and discussions with professional advisors?**
- At the time he/she joins the practice?
_____
- When he/she becomes a stockholder?
_____

☐ **Procedure by which a new physician becomes a stockholder:**
- Waiting time _____
- Terms of the purchase _____
- Assets included _____
- At what point an equal stockholder? ___
_____

☐ **Does the practice own its own building?** _____

☐ **Are there provisions for the new physician to buy into the building?** _____
- Share of interest _____
- Terms of buy-in _____

☐ **How are accounts receivable handled?**
- When buying in _____
- When paying off an existing stockholder

_____

☐ **How are termination benefits handled?**
- Stock interest _____
- Receivables _____

☐ **Does the firm have a relationship with:**
- Banker? _____
- Insurance agent? _____
- Financial planner? _____
- Realtor? _____
- Stockbroker? _____

☐ **Does the firm's attorney handle estate planning for the new physician?** _____
Who pays the fee? _____

☐ **Does the firm's accountant handle tax returns for the new physician?** _____
Who pays the fee? _____

☐ **Is there an employment contract governing each of the above items?** _____
Will it be available for signature prior to employment?

_____

ABOUT THE AUTHORS

TODD D. BRAMSON, CFP®, CHFC®, CLU®

Certified Financial Planner™ practitioner Todd D. Bramson has been working in the field of financial planning for more than thirty-five years. He is an Editorial Consultant with *Medical Economics* magazine and has contributed to many articles.

An exceptional teacher, as well as a motivating author and speaker, Todd has been quoted in numerous financial publications and has spent several years as the financial expert on the local *NBC Live* 5:00 p.m. news broadcast. He has spoken at the annual conference of the prestigious Million Dollar Round Table (MDRT), The Premier Association of Financial Professionals™.[19]

Todd's belief, "If the trust is there, the miles don't matter," has earned him devoted clients, not only in his hometown of Madison, Wisconsin, but in most states throughout the country. Along with achieving all the designations expected of a trusted financial professional, he is committed to keeping abreast of the developments in his field and playing an active role in his community. Todd is active in The Evans Scholars Alumni Foundation and Blackhawk Country Club, and he is a director with Western Golf Association. He is also a member of Verandah Club in Fort Myers, Florida, and The Outpost Club.

In addition, Todd is the founder and president of Bramson and Associates LLC. Information about his company, philosophy, and services are at www.toddbramson.com. He is the author and creator of the *Real-Life Financial Planning* book series, which now includes sixteen books, with more than 35,000 copies in print.

---

19. See the "Additional Disclosures" section at the back of this book for affiliated disclosures.

WESLEY R. SHARP

Wesley R. Sharp is an independent financial advisor with a digital and virtual practice that allows him to consult and counsel his clients throughout the United States. Wesley joined North Star in 2013 and immediately immersed himself into the well-established Medical Division at North Star. He specializes in working with physicians, dentists, and pharmacists. This has led to his extensive knowledge on financial strategies during the grueling residency and fellowship stages, as well as techniques on how to become financially independent once in practice. As a result of this unique practice and experience, Wes was the perfect addition to cowrite and contribute to the third edition of this book, *Real-Life Financial Planning for Physicians*.

In addition to partnering with Jon and Todd, Wes has built a powerful team of field experts to provide world-class service and wisdom to his clients. Wes focuses on comprehensive, fee-based financial planning in his practice. This allows him to provide customized guidance on the unique financial scenarios that physicians and other medical professionals face. This includes counseling and advising on student loans, tax-efficient investment strategies, retirement preparation, asset protection, risk management, education funding, physician-specific home buying, partner buy-ins, and much more. Creating this team has allowed Wes and his joint practice to service and maintain clients across the country and to welcome new clients.

Wes currently lives in Minneapolis to be close to his family. When he isn't working, you can either find Wes with his beautiful wife, Alexa, chasing their two children, Ella, and Bennett around or out on the golf course, likely searching in the woods for his tee shot.

JON C. YLINEN

Jon C. Ylinen is a full partner at North Star Resource Group. He is an independent comprehensive financial consultant and wealth manager who has a national-reaching practice with clients in forty-one states. He currently works with several hundred physicians, starting as early as their final year of medical school, through residency, fellowship, in practice, and continuing through retirement.

His practice offers customized financial planning* on an expansive basis. In 2017, he produced the most independent client plans throughout Securian's entire network of more than 1,100 financial advisors, and he ranked second-highest in plans produced in both 2015 and 2016. Jon's passion for this goal-driven planning is rooted in the belief that financial services and asset management should revolve around a plan that targets the client's goals, be independent in nature, and be very well-rounded in its approach. This strategy focuses on establishing emergency reserves, thoughtful debt management, strategic asset protection*, and risk management, along with tactical wealth accumulation geared toward what matters most to the client.

In addition to his private client work, Jon's academic work started with being a co-author of the book *Real-Life Financial Planning for Physicians* and moved on to pioneering financial columns such as the "Financial Focus" column for *Review of Ophthalmology* and "EM$ and Sense" for *Emergency Medicine Magazine*, in addition to his contributions to numerous articles for Medical Economics. He currently concentrates this side of his work to his ongoing column at *Physician's Money Digest.*

Outside of his financial-planning practice, Jon and his wife, Alyssa, enjoy spending time with their children, traveling, and training for triathlons.

---

*Financial planning is a fee-based service. Separate from the financial plan and an advisor's role as financial planner, an advisor may recommend the purchase of specific investment or insurance products or accounts. These product recommendations are not part of the financial plan, and clients are under no obligation to follow them.

Contributing Author

ROBERT KAUFER, JD

Robert Kaufer has more than twenty years of experience as a practicing attorney, working primarily in the areas of simple and complex estate planning, business and contract law, probate law, and residential real estate law. Bob earned his law degree from Hamline University School of Law and his MBA from the University of St. Thomas. He, his wife, and their two children reside in St. Paul.

Bob's legal philosophy is to educate clients about their options and then help them make the best choices to meet their unique goals and objectives. Robert is not affiliated with CRI Securities or Securian Financial Services Inc.

888-711-4524
www.robertkaufer.com

NORTH STAR
Resource Group

Todd D. Bramson, CFP˚, ChFC˚, CLU˚
North Star Resource Group
2945 Triverton Pike Drive, #200
Madison, WI 53711
Direct: 1-608-271-3669, ext. 218
todd.bramson@northstarfinancial.com

Wesley R. Sharp
North Star Resource Group
2701 University Avenue, SE
Minneapolis, MN 55431
Direct: 1-612-617-6067
wes.sharp@northstarfinancial.com

Jon C. Ylinen
North Star Resource Group
2945 Triverton Pike Drive, #200
Madison, WI 53711
Direct: 1-608-271-3669
jon@northstarfinancial.com

ADDITIONAL DISCLOSURES

Million Dollar Round Table (MDRT) is an independent membership organization of life insurance and financial service professionals. Membership levels are based on commissions, premiums, or fees generated within a year from investment and insurance products. Members must apply annually and pay a fee. Members must be members in good standing of a professional association that has met the following criteria: in existence at least 2 years, has 100 or more members, must be a nonprofit organization, must have a code of ethics and an effective means of dealing with breaches of its code. Members must also adhere to the MDRT Code of Ethics. Working with this advisor is not a guarantee of future financial results. Investors should conduct their own evaluation.

Variable life insurance, variable annuities, and mutual funds are sold only by prospectus. The prospectus contains important information about the product's charges and expenses, as well as the risks and other information associated with the product. You should carefully consider the risks and investment charges of a specific product before investing. You should always read the prospectus carefully before investing.

This book contains a lot of information and investment/planning strategies. Keeping in mind that everyone's financial situation is different, the strategies and concepts discussed within this book may not be appropriate for everyone. You should meet with your financial, legal, and tax advisors before implementing any financial, legal, or tax strategy.

The tax concepts that are addressed in this book are current as of 2018. Tax laws change frequently, and any tax concept addressed in this book might not be applicable after 2018.